The Field Placement Survival Guide

What You Need to Know to Get the Most From Your Social Work Practicum

edited by
Linda May Grobman, ACSW, LSW
editor, THE NEW SOCIAL WORKER®

Best of THE NEW SOCIAL WORKER®
A White Hat Communications Book Series

THE FIELD PLACEMENT SURVIVAL GUIDE
What You Need to Know to Get the Most From Your Social Work Practicum

edited by Linda May Grobman

Published by:

P.O. Box 5390 • Harrisburg, PA 17110-0390
717-238-3787 (voice)
717-238-2090 (fax)
http://www.socialworker.com

Library of Congress Cataloging-in-Publication Data

The field placement survival guide : what you need to know to get the most from your social work practicum / edited by Linda May Grobman.
     p. cm. — (Best of the new social worker ; 2)
Includes bibliographical references and index.
   ISBN 1-929109-10-5 (pbk.)
1. Social service—Field work. I. Grobman, Linda May. II. Series.
HV11 .F453 2002
361.3'07'23—dc21

                                        2001006297

Contents

Acknowledgments

Thank you to all the contributors to this book for sharing their experience and wisdom with those who are new to the social work profession.

Thank you to the educators and field instructors who are "in the trenches" every day, helping students survive the field placement experience.

Thank you to Jan Ligon who, in addition to being a long-time supporter of and advisor to *THE NEW SOCIAL WORKER*, read an early manuscript of this book and provided his expert opinion and suggestions.

Thank you to Gary Grobman, my husband, for his encouragement, as well as his proofreading and editing skills.

About the Editor

Linda May Grobman, ACSW, LSW, is editor and publisher of *THE NEW SOCIAL WORKER®* magazine. She received her MSW from the University of Georgia and worked as a social worker in mental health and medical settings. She also served as a staff member for two state chapters of the National Association of Social Workers (NASW). She is editor of the book *DAYS IN THE LIVES OF SOCIAL WORKERS* and co-author (with Gary B. Grant) of *THE SOCIAL WORKER'S INTERNET HANDBOOK*.

About the Contributors

Angela Allen, BSW, graduated from Appalachian State University in May 1997. As a child protective services social worker at Ashe County Department of Social Services in North Carolina, she has found it more important than ever to count her blessings every day.

Denise Anderson, Ph.D., MSW, is Assistant Professor of Social Work at Shippensburg University in Shippensburg, PA. She is a former field instructor and was a faculty liaison for eight years.

Marla Berg-Weger, Ph.D., LCSW, is Associate Professor and Director of Practicum at Saint Louis University School of Social Service. She has been involved in social work field education for two decades, serving in both field and university settings. Her scholarly achievements include works in field education, family, aging, and interdisciplinary education.

Julie Birkenmaier, MSW, LCSW, is Assistant Clinical Professor at Saint Louis University School of Social Service. Her responsibilities include serving as a field instructor for students and teaching Integrative Seminar courses for the BSW and MSW programs. She is currently pursuing a Ph.D. in Political Science.

Heather Coleman, Ph.D., MSW, BSW, is Associate Professor with the Faculty of Social Work, University of Calgary, in Canada. She has written in the areas of family practice, family violence, social work education, and addiction.

Don Collins, Ph.D., MSW, BSW, is Professor with the Faculty of Social Work, University of Calgary, in Canada. He has written three books on the social work practicum and a book on family social work. He teaches social work practice skills.

Joan Ferry DiGiulio, Ph.D., LISW, is Chair and Professor at the Department of Social Work, Youngstown State University in Youngstown, Ohio. She has been a social work educator for 25 years, specializing in families and children. She has authored numerous articles on field education, loss, and adoption.

Katherine M. Dunlap, Ph.D., ACSW, is Associate Professor and Director of the Inter-Institutional MSW Program at the University of North Carolina at Chapel Hill. Her research interests include pre-school education, family support programs, adult education, and school social work.

Charles E. Floyd, Ph.D., LCSW, is Field Coordinator and Associate Professor at the MSW Program, California State University, Stanislaus.

Sondra J. Fogel, Ph.D., MSSW, ACSW, is Associate Professor at the University of South Florida School of Social Work. Her research includes issues in field education, community development and capacity building, and homelessness.

Erlene Grise-Owens, Ed.D., LCSW, MSW, is Assistant Professor and Director of Field Education in the Department of Social Work, Spalding University, Louisville, KY. She has practice experience in diverse areas, including child welfare, mental health, and faith-based social services.

Linda Hagerty, MSW, LCSW, is Field Coordinator at West Virginia University Division of Social Work, School of Social Work and Public Administration, Morgantown, WV. In addition to coordinating field placements for BSW and MSW students, she trains field instructors.

Shavone Hamilton, CSW, received her MSW from Fordham University Graduate School of Social Services. She is a clinician at the mental health clinic of the AIDS Center of Queens County in New York. She specializes in individual, family, and group work with addicted and HIV/AIDS affected populations.

Randee Huber, MSW, is employed as a hospice social worker. She did her field placement in 1997-1998 at an inpatient Post Traumatic Stress Disorder (PTSD) program in a VA Medical Center.

Pamela J. Huggins, LCSW, ACSW, is Coordinator of Field Instruction in the BSW program at Indiana University. In her work with employed master's level students, she gained insight into developing practica that both protected the educational learning and the opportunity to expand knowledge, skills, and service to their current employers.

Wendy K. Langley, MSW, was a BSW student when she wrote her article on being observed, which appears in this book. She received her BSW from Louisiana College and her MSW from Washington University's George Warren Brown School of Social Work. She is a social worker at a transitional housing program for homeless families.

Jan Ligon, PhD, LCSW, is Assistant Professor and BSW Program Director with the Georgia State University School of Social Work. He serves as a member of THE NEW SOCIAL WORKER's Editorial Advisory Board.

Denice Goodrich Liley, Ph.D., ACSW, Diplomat in Social Work, is Assistant Professor of social work at Boise State University. She has more than twenty years of practice experience as a social worker.

Betsy C. Mistek, BSSW, was a senior at Minnesota State University, Mankato when she wrote "Listen Up." She graduated in December 1999 and works at a nonprofit agency serving adults with disabilities, focusing on community-based employment.

Susan T. Ross, Ed.D., MSW, ACSW, LCSW, is Associate Professor and Coordinator of Field Instruction at Aurora University, George Williams College School of Social Work, in Aurora, Illinois. She has conducted field seminars and practice classes for both BSW and MSW students, and is a former field instructor and career counselor.

Mona C. S. Schatz, DSW, is Professor and Director of the Education and Research Institute for Fostering Families at Colorado State University. She has served as Director of Field Education at CSU, and has examined outcomes for field education within a generalist and advanced generalist social work perspective. She introduced the use of portfolios to the undergraduate program in 1995, and later to the graduate program.

Dean Schneck, MSSW, ACSW, Clinical Professor Emeritus from the University of Wisconsin-Madison, is recently retired and living in rural Southern Oregon. He was Field Director and faculty member at the UW-Madison for over 25 years. He was instrumental in the founding of the Field Work Symposium and the Commission on Field Education within the Council on Social Work Education and published with Bart Grossman and Urania Glassman FIELD EDUCATION IN SOCIAL WORK: CONTEMPORARY ISSUES AND TRENDS (Kendall/Hunt, 1991). Other interests include generalist practice, child welfare, and criminal justice.

Sarah Simon, MSW, was a senior social work student at Colorado State University when she wrote her article on the portfolio approach with Mona Schatz. She worked with Dr. Schatz on the first evaluation of portfolios at the BSW level and later examined how graduate and undergraduate students viewed their portfolio development process.

Gary S. Stofle, LISW, CCDCIIIE, ACSW, is a Team Leader at North Central Mental Health Center in Columbus, OH. He is author of the book *CHOOSING AN ONLINE THERAPIST: A STEP-BY-STEP GUIDE TO FINDING PROFESSIONAL HELP ON THE WEB* (White Hat Communications, 2001).

Kimberly Strom-Gottfried, Ph.D., MSW, LISW, is Interim Dean at the University of North Carolina at Chapel Hill School of Social Work. Building on her practice experience in mental health, Dr. Strom-Gottfried has been an educator on both the BSW and MSW levels, teaching social work practice, policy, and management. She is a former chair of the NASW National Committee on Inquiry and has written extensively about social work education, ethics, and managed care.

Gregory R. Versen, MSSW, ACSW, is Associate Professor at James Madison University in Harrisonburg, VA, where he has served as Director of Field Placement since 1988.

Cheryl Waites, Ed.D., MSW, ACSW, is Associate Professor and Academic Coordinator at the North Carolina State University Social Work Program. She was previously on the faculty at UNC Pembroke, where she was the Coordinator of Field Education. She has published in the areas of child welfare, African American adolescents and elders, cultural competence, practice methods, and social work education.

Joseph Walsh, Ph.D., LCSW, is Associate Professor of Social Work at Virginia Commonwealth University. He has also been a clinical practitioner for over 20 years. He teaches courses in clinical practice, generalist practice, and human behavior. His area of special interest is serious mental illness, and he is working on a book on endings in clinical practice.

Jim Ward, MSW, is Director of Field Instruction for the College of Social Work, University of South Carolina, in Columbia, SC.

Althea Webb, MSSW, CSW, is Director of Field Education and an Assistant Professor at Murray State University, Murray, KY. She is pursuing a Ph.D. in higher education at the University of Kentucky. Her dissertation will focus on the historical development of social work education for African Americans in Kentucky from 1921-1951.

Ruth T. Weinzettle, MSW, LCSW, is Field Placement Coordinator at Louisiana College in Pineville, LA. As a direct practitioner for 13 years, she sometimes supervised social work students.

Introduction

Field placement—as I remember it, it is one of the most exciting and exhilarating parts of a formal social work education. It is also one of the most challenging. It allows you, the student, to put into practice the concepts, theories, and skills you have learned in the classroom. It puts you in the position of "practicing" with live clients. It gives you room to explore and grow as a budding professional. More than anything else, it requires you to look inside yourself—to examine yourself, your abilities, your reactions, and your suitability as a social worker. It can be invigorating, and it can be extremely difficult.

Many of the chapters in this book started out as articles in *THE NEW SOCIAL WORKER,* the magazine for social work students and recent graduates. Field placement articles have been a regular item in *THE NEW SOCIAL WORKER* since it began in 1994. With the help of members of the SW-FIELD-WORK electronic mailing list and the many field placement experts I have met through the years, the magazine has served to provide useful, practical information for students undergoing the field experience.

Field placement—regardless of the setting or time—involves universal issues for all social work students. Those issues are reflected in these articles, which are presented here as part of the "Best of THE NEW SOCIAL WORKER" book series. These articles represent the "best" that educators who work day-to-day with field placement students have to offer.

The title of this book is *THE FIELD PLACEMENT SURVIVAL GUIDE. Is field placement something that I must survive?* you may ask. What does that mean? I conducted a survey on *THE NEW SOCIAL WORKER's* Web site to help name this book. The title with the word "survival" in it won hands down. I suspect that the reason for this is that those who have already gone through the practicum experience *do* feel as if they have survived.

I sure felt that way. As an MSW student who wanted to enter the mental health field, I couldn't have landed a more perfect placement. I interviewed and was accepted at a large family service agency in a major metropolitan area. I was placed at the agency's branch office in my neighborhood. There were social work students from prestigious schools around the country, and we would meet each week for group supervision and learning. I would be working alongside and learning from some of the social work leaders in the area.

My field instructor became a trusted and important mentor in my budding social work career. She pushed me to constantly examine myself and my work with the agency's clients. The experience was intense. I often felt as if my inner being was under a magnifying glass, for everyone (especially my supervisor, other staff, fellow students in the agency, and even clients) to see.

The other students in the agency were important to my learning, as well. In our weekly group supervision/training sessions, we shared ideas, experiences, and concerns. We learned from each other, and we benefitted from participating in a group, much as our group therapy participants might benefit. I remember that I shared an office with a student from another school. The interaction with her was invaluable, as we were able to informally compare notes.

The practicum was all I could hope for and more. It was one of the most difficult experiences of my life (and certainly of my education), and I wouldn't have had it any other way. I learned, I grew, and I survived.

You may feel this way, too. It's not that anyone is purposely putting you through a "survival" experience, like college fraternity "hazing" or those "reality-based" TV shows. It's just that learning to practice social work is hard work. The intense self-examination is a necessary part of learning to work with others. Putting theory into practice may not come as easily as you thought it would. You may feel uncomfortable with "not knowing"—a concept Manfred Melcher discusses in his book *BECOMING A SOCIAL WORKER* (another book in this series).

You may (and probably will) bump into some challenges along the way. As my graduate school field instructor told me, "If being a social worker was so easy, you wouldn't need a social work education to do it." You are becoming a professional in a highly demanding field, and it takes some work to get there.

The chapters in this book can help you get through those bumpy spots, keep moving through your placement, and get to the other side—being a full-fledged, successful social work professional.

Each chapter was originally accepted as an article for *THE NEW SOCIAL WORKER* because of its practicality and usefulness to social work students. (A few new ones were added, as well.) As I read through each one again in editing this book, I realized that this collection contains a goldmine of information. I also realized that some of the chapters repeat what others have said, while a few may contradict each other. I leave it to you to read each point of view and use it as you see fit.

Discuss the material in this book with your classmates, your field instructor, your field liaison, and others involved in your field placement. And sing loudly and clearly, as Gloria Gaynor did in the '70s disco song, "I will survive!"

Linda May Grobman, ACSW, LSW

Preface

What Every Social Work Student Should Know About Field Placement

by Dean Schneck, MSSW, ACSW

As each school term begins, thousands of students across the U.S. and Canada enter social work education programs, both at the baccalaureate and master's levels. The vast majority will be entering a field practicum in the community. For most students, this will comprise their introduction to professional practice, while some will enter the field practicum with work experience. For all, field education provides a major opportunity for the development of professional identity and skills, the practical application of theoretical concepts, and an arena for the integration of life and work experience.

Field learning has historically held special significance for students by virtue of its inherent authenticity (i.e. responsibility in the "real world" to help people with "real problems") and by its fulfillment of students' needs to assume a professional role and try out their skills. Across North America, students will be working with young children, adolescents, families, and the elderly. They will be assisting the mentally ill, the homeless, and disabled persons. They will come to grips with major social problems, such as substance abuse, violence, and poverty. Social work students, with professional and academic guidance, will make substantial contributions to others as they learn.

This is not to diminish the value of classroom learning. Knowledge, methods, and ideas learned in the classroom enable students to practice thoughtfully and purposefully in the field. Field education, when done well, provides an opportunity for the application of content learned in the class-room. Field education should provide students with an op-portunity to develop conceptual (analytic, problem-solving, and organizational) skills, as well as interactional skills (in-terviewing, counseling, group work, advocacy, and resource networking). These are some common goals across all pro-grams, though the field education model and delivery struc-ture will vary.

There is most always a field office comprised of a field director or coordinator and field staff or faculty who have responsibility for placement, monitoring, problem-solving, and evaluation of students. A group learning experience is usually integral to the field experience. This may take the form of an integrative seminar taught on campus, a series of workshops or seminars held over the course of a semes-ter, or a field unit seminar held as part of a field unit or field teaching center. Many schools have developed field learn-ing centers located in large agencies, such as hospitals, mental health centers, or as part of a community center.

Expectations

Though the educational models may vary, there are ex-pectations that are generally shared among social work pro-grams and reinforced by accreditation standards from the Council on Social Work Education (CSWE). You have a right to expect of the field agency and educational program:

- a planned and structured learning experience that pro-vides you with the opportunity to learn social work prac-tice through providing service to individuals, families, and/or groups.
- a clear statement of your learning and performance ex-pectations from the educational program and an orien-tation to the field agency, staff, and service programs.
- consistent professional and educational supervision throughout the course of your field placement, which would include constructive criticism, evaluation, and supportive resources.
- an opportunity for individual and group learning expe-riences for the application and integration of classroom content with field activities.

- respectful and ethical treatment by field instructors and faculty who take a genuine interest in the quality of your learning experience. This would include availability in crisis situations, as well as regular supervision, and a willingness to advocate for you to secure a good learning opportunity.
- an evaluation process or conference that provides you with both positive feedback and constructive criticism.

The field agency and educational program have a right to expect:

- that you express your perceived learning needs, career goals and interests, and relevant background information with clarity.
- that you participate actively in the placement process, including completion of preplacement interviews, meeting prerequisites, necessary paperwork, and so on.
- that you perform ethically and competently in all field assignments to the best of your ability.
- that you cooperate fully with your field instructor and faculty liaison, especially including the incorporation of their feedback and criticism.
- that you regard the needs of those you serve with the utmost care and attention and, in general, function as a "good citizen" of the agency and community.

Problem Solving

Inevitably, some students over the course of the year will encounter problems in their field placements. These may be due to unanticipated events in the field agency, such as program or staff changes, funding cutbacks, or supervisory problems, or they may be engendered by a personal crisis or illness, or they may be seen in performance problems of students. Both students and field instructors have recourse to the social work department or school in the event of any of these problems, and it is always better that they be resolved sooner rather than later. Therefore, if a student is not receiving field assignments in a timely fashion or is not receiving consistent and quality supervision, he or she should bring this matter to the attention of the faculty liaison or advisor, or to the field director. Remember, you are entitled to an adequate opportunity to demonstrate your abilities and meet the requirements of the practicum.

It is also incumbent on the field instructor and the faculty liaison to deal with performance deficits of the student. Students are entitled to specific feedback regarding their performance, and adequate time and resources to improve and complete the requirements of the practicum. In most instances, students can improve their performance, given an openness to critical feedback and supervisory support. In those relatively few instances in which students perform very poorly in placement, field instructors and faculty should act to protect the needs of the client, even if this means replacing the student.

Achieving Excellence

Learning expectations, contracts, and field manuals will structure the opportunity, inform you and others of what's expected, and should assure good supervision. These provide the foundation for your learning. The rest is up to you. It is very important for field students to be active and assertive adult learners. Students who demonstrate initiative and perseverance throughout the field placement will usually receive a wider array of experiences and more autonomy. Suggestions include:

- being a "quick study" of the agency's mission, client populations, and service programs, even those in which you are not directly involved;
- seeking out reading and other learning resources;
- developing a working understanding of agency policies and limitations;
- being well-prepared for client interviews, staff meetings, case presentations, court hearings, and so on;
- presenting thoughtful and well-written case notes, resource referrals, court reports, and professional correspondence;
- having on-time follow-through with any stated or implied commitment to clients or agency staff;
- going the extra mile to think and behave professionally; and

- being a good day-to-day professional colleague to agency staff, fellow students, and other social workers in the community.

The foregoing will require extra effort and time, discipline, and hard work. Such is the cost of excellence—the alternative is mediocrity.

Developing Character

Top social work professionals, the kind that command the respect and admiration of their colleagues and clients, evidence a great deal of character. By character, I mean the personal integration of professional values and personal attributes. Such character traits as honesty, courage, integrity, and generosity are fundamental to the practice activities of students and staff alike as they strive for better answers, more effective and humane methods, and greater competence.

Another important character trait is the willingness to engage in critical self-evaluation throughout one's career, beginning in the field placement. You can learn to reflect carefully upon your intentions and performance, to discern areas of strength and weakness, and then to use supervision to validate your reflections and improve your practice. It is far better to self-reflect and self-correct than to erect barriers and rationalizations for deficits that may later require the intervention of others to correct.

You will meet and work with some social workers and faculty who will inspire you, others who will disappoint you, and others at different points in between. Social work, as in all professions, includes practitioners of varying degrees of commitment, talent, and competence. Because field education usually occurs early in one's career, it affords you a chance to observe and scrutinize not only yourself, but also the agencies and the profession. It is a good time to decide what kind of professional social worker you will be.

None of us is ever a finished product. It is a crucial ethic of professional practice that we all continue to develop and expand our abilities throughout our careers. The social problems we face and the people who depend on us demand nothing less. You are the next generation of professional social workers and you will face very difficult and challenging problems, in some ways more difficult and complex than those faced by those of us who have gone before you. Social work is not only a noble endeavor, but a necessary endeavor for a humane and just society. It is worth doing and doing well.

We have all had the support and guidance of a teacher, a field supervisor, or a mentor; and in due course, you will provide the same to an eager student. But for now, this is your time. Work hard, learn well, and you will make a difference. We will be there to help you along the way.

Want to Know More?

Especially for Students

Rogers, G., Collins, D., Barlow, C., & Grinnell, R. M. (2000). *Guide to the social work practicum: A team approach.* Itaska, IL: F. E. Peacock.

Royce, D., Dhooper, S. S., & Rompf, E. L. (1993). *Field instruction: A guide for social work students.* New York: Longman.

General References

Schneck, D., Grossman, B., & Glassman, U. (1991). *Field education in social work: Contemporary issues and trends.* Dubuque, IA: Kendall/Hunt.

Sheafor, B. W., & Jenkins, L. E. (1982). *Quality field instruction in social work.* New York: Longman.

Bogo, M., & Vayda, E. (1987). *The practice of field instruction in social work: Theory and process—with an annotated bibliography.* Toronto: The University of Toronto Press.

PART I

CHOOSING YOUR PLACEMENT

PART I: CHOOSING YOUR PLACEMENT

Everyone wants a great practicum, but what does that mean? Is it a practicum that is close to where you live, or that exposes you to a different geographic area? Is it in your desired field of practice, or does it let you experience a variety of client populations? Is it easy, or is it more difficult and challenging? Does it allow you autonomy, or does it provide close supervision and guidance? Will it lead to a job, or will it let you stay at your current job?

It could be any of these, or none of these. The factors that make a practicum great for you might make it undesirable for someone else. Some people suggest that you talk to students who have done practica in an agency before making a decision. That is not necessarily bad advice, and it can in fact be very good advice, as long as you remember that you still need to take into account your own needs and goals.

How does the decision for practicum placement happen, anyway? It varies from school to school, with some assigning the practicum site with little student input and others providing an interviewing process similar to a job interview.

Whatever the process at your school, it will be helpful if you decide (with the input of the faculty liaison, your advisor, and others) what your goals are. What do you want and need to accomplish? What are your career goals? How will your field placement experience help you reach your professional aspirations?

The decision is not an easy one, and it is one that will have a great impact on your life as a social worker. Make it wisely!

1

The Road to Practicum: I Want A Great One!

Denice Goodrich Liley, Ph.D., ACSW

The pre-requisite classes and much of the formal coursework are nearly completed. The opportunities to *practice* the knowledge and skills are within reach. Out into *the field* sounds so ominous. Where? Which agency or organization? With whom? The search begins: Practicum!

How do social work students choose a field practicum? Most importantly, the choice does need to be the best choice possible. And, of course, every student wants the *best* practicum experience or at least a field practicum experience that is really good! Does this sound familiar?

How common it is for students to visit the field practicum office at the beginning of their search for a practicum, and to then have the practicum director tell them, "But *all* the field practicum sites really *are* good." As a social work student, your thoughts, more likely than not, are, "No! No! I want the really *great* one, the special one that is kept for the most special students . . . not just a *good* practicum for just anybody!!" Students often feel that really special field practicums are kept on a shelf or in a file and given out subjectively: the special practicum for the special student. As a student, perhaps you want to proclaim, "I *am* special." "Listen to me! Ask others." "I'll demonstrate and prove it." Many students leave with a lingering feeling about how to *snag* that illusively vague, *perfect* practicum.

How do social work students find the perfect field practicum that is the GREAT ONE? It really is not a secret, nor are they kept hidden away. The real question is how to acquire a particular field practicum for a particular person. The answer is found in the uniquely individual nature of the *best in practicum.* A great practicum is a match between the student, the placement setting, and the specific educational objectives and outcomes for that student.

Student interests that should be considered are : **Who**—What populations of people. **Where**—level of social work practice—individual, family, households, groups, or the larger community. And **what**—the challenges clients will be experiencing. It is helpful to consider your life experiences. It is also important to consider the individual strengths and challenges each student brings with them to the practicum experience.

Important agency information to consider includes: What agencies does your particular University partner with (private as well as public, profit, not for profit)? How does the agency's philosophy in delivery of services coincide with those the university supports? Does the agency have any specific requirements that are different from the University's?

In regard to educational objectives and outcomes as a specific social work student, consider the following: What types of tasks as an individual student do you need in order to round out your educational experiences? Will this practicum experience provide a challenge, build and support your individual educational needs, and provide opportunities to expand and develop new knowledge, values, and skills?

As overwhelming as it may seem, the first step to being placed in the most appropriate practicum begins by doing a lot of individual work. It is not solely the field practicum director's responsibility to ensure that every student engage in the best field practicum. It is imperative that social work students assume pro-active responsibility for and partner in this adventure. And a pragmatic method to set the course in action does exist:

Approaching Selection

First, do your homework as to YOU! Some common questions to consider include: What do you want, expect, and feel you need in a field practicum? What are your long-term career goals? Do you have any specific ideas of the groups of people you want to work with or specifically do NOT want to work with? What life experiences, work experiences have you had? What do you think could make you a better social worker? Many of these are questions only you can answer, and it is important that you take time to be reflective about them. You don't want to leave to chance or make a hasty, last minute decision about what very well could be one of the most important decisions in your social work education.

Numerous books are available that provide information about considerations in selecting a practicum. The titles of a few of these books are included at the end of this article as suggested readings. Many of these books provide activities to assist you in your self-reflective process and in the field practicum selection. Additionally, the books illuminate common field practicum experiences of former social work students. Many of the books not only provide questions for you, but they also include questions to use when evaluating agencies and field supervisors for potential field practicum placements.

Seek out and interview social work students currently in field placements. Explore their opinions about what they like about the field sites where they are working. These students are in the front lines, so to speak, and they are involved in the most current social work experiences. And because only a year prior they were where you are today, they can most closely relate to your concerns. Do they have any suggestions or comments about what they might do differently? How did they go about selecting their particular agency for their field practicum? Current social work students can provide a wealth of information that cannot be obtained anywhere else.

Speak with social work faculty. This includes those individuals who have taught your formal course work classes, your advisor, and possibly any faculty you know to have had research or practice experience in the fields you are considering. Social work faculties frequently serve as liaisons to field practicum agencies or may perform community service in a wide variety of agencies, and could provide valuable input regarding the various agencies. Additionally, they may be able to share feedback about the experiences other students have had in various agencies over the years. An added benefit of consulting social work faculty is that, if they know you well, they may be able to address and be candid about your strengths and/or challenges. They can be the source of insightful and objective information for you to consider in your evaluation of field practicum.

Be sure to consult your school's field practicum manual. This manual contains the formal policy and procedure for your school's field practicum program. It will provide a broad perspective, not only from the school's view, but also for agencies, and at the individual student level. The field practicum manual defines roles and responsibilities for school, agency, and student.

Schedule a visit with the practicum director in your school's field placement office. If you have done your homework as to your particulars, identified where and what current social work students are actively engaged in field practicums, spoken with other social work faculty, and consulted the field practicum manual, this visit can be a very productive meeting. It is important to be realistic and to have established a fit between your expectations and reality. The social work field practicum is an initiatory experience in your professional career. It is NOT the *end* of your education. Hopefully, you will continue to experience many rewarding and challenging opportunities upon graduation. It is important not to expect that your social work field experience will give you everything.

Narrow your list of possibilities for social work field practicum, and visit some agencies. It is important not to waste your time and the agency's time if you know you are not interested in the agency or if for other reasons, you'd never do your practicum in that area. On the other hand, it is important to for you to think broadly enough to consider some alternatives as to client systems and agencies that you can have a learning experience. Risking the unknown could very well open up new avenues that you had never considered.

It is important to be prepared when doing your agency visits; that is, be prompt, punctual, and professional. You need to know what the agency does (who they serve and broad terms of the delivery of services) so you can focus your time on learning what a social work student might actually do at this agency. Questions to consider are: What are a few basic experiences that social work students have at your agency? What do you feel is the most rewarding part of social work within your agency? What is the most challenging? How is supervision handled? What types of students succeed in your agency? It is always beneficial to send a thank you note following your interview, regardless of your decision. The social work practice community is very small, and you never know when your paths with these agencies could cross again. Leaving them your best impression always serves you well.

Summary

No matter what your selection is, most students look upon the social work field practicum experience as the single most learning experience of their educational careers. All students must meet certain requirements to participate in a field practicum, and all agencies must meet certain criteria in order to function as field practicum sites for social work education. Included in these expectations are very specific educational outcomes linked to the university, to the student, and to the agency. Additionally, the field practicum is designed to allow for individual student learning through personal goals and objectives. The key is to identify particulars, and to aim for them. Be pro-active and student-focused... Advocate for yourself. Gain information. Guide the course of events rather than coasting. This will ensure a **GREAT** practicum, not merely a *good* one!

Suggested Reading

Cochrain, S. F., & Hanley, M. M. (1999). *Learning through field: A developmental approach.* Boston: Allyn and Bacon.

Collins, D., Tomlison, B., & Grinnell, R. M. (1992). *The social work practicum: A student guide.* Itasca, IL: F. E. Peacock.

Horejsi, C. J., & Garthwait, C. L. (1999). *The social work practicum: A guide and workbook for students.* Boston: Allyn and Bacon.

Rothman, J. C. (2000). *Stepping out into the field: A field work manual for social work students.* Boston: Allyn and Bacon.

Royse, D., Dhooper, S. S., & Rompf, E. L. (1999). *Field instruction: A guide for social work students.* New York: Longman.

2

Choosing a Field Placement—Wisely!

by Linda Hagerty, MSW, LCSW

Choosing a field placement can be a minefield for students at times. We often repeat the phrase—finding a good "fit" between student needs and field site possibilities. Yet, understanding what that actually means can be difficult for a student to know or understand.

Intrinsic vs. Peripheral

Many times, a student is worried and feeling pressured about financial survival. Sometimes, this leads students to make field placement choices that explode in their faces, or lead to lack of satisfaction in less obvious ways. For example, a student was very concerned about a car that was on its last legs, about her father's surgery, about taking out a loan when she already had student loans piled up from undergrad school, and so on. Sound familiar?

So, after interviewing, she passed up the choice that "felt right, and looked best" for a second choice which did not require much use of car. As the mismatch was discovered, growing out of three very stressful weeks early in the placement, we talked about what she was learning about herself and her decision-making process. How would she choose a life partner? Would she make the choice based on whether their route to work would make her transportation burden easier? Would she choose a life partner to facilitate her own career ambitions? Would she choose a life partner to make her life more convenient? Of course not, or at least, if she saw a friend allowing such peripheral motives to influence a lifelong personal commitment, she would recognize the potential for disaster that might lie ahead.

So it goes with field placement choices. The match between student and internship site is not a lifelong personal commitment, but there are some distinct parallels. The choice needs to be made based on careful thinking about the interests, personal style, and career readiness of the student; the practice opportunities the field site offers; and the style and expertise of the field instructor. The *intrinsic aspects* of the choice, rather than the peripheral life issues, need to be the first and central concern while making the decision about "fit." After those are identified, field coordinators work with students to solve problems related to the life issues and secondary considerations students are understandably concerned with.

Another version of the financial pressure that may influence students' choices, perhaps in a negative way, is the presence of a stipend or the graduate assistantship. We all see students gravitating to those placements that offer some financial support and wish we could provide them for all students! One student had a graduate assistantship at the school, which he wanted to keep. Therefore, he chose a field placement site that was located conveniently for him to manage both. Very soon, the placement "blew up," possibly for multiple reasons, but the "convenience factor" was certainly a major aspect of the whole.

Sometimes, the presence of a stipend enhances an already positive *intrinsic* fit. We all use such incentives, particularly to draw students into crucial fields where more professional expertise is desirable, such as in child welfare. When the student has a sufficiently strong *intrinsic* interest in the field of practice, these incentives can tip the scales enough to influence one direction over several possible choices. However, when the match is too artificial, the incentive can backfire.

Confusing Choices

Confusing choices abound, even when we put aside the influence of the peripheral life issues and try to sort out the factors that are within the intrinsic arena. Social work programs vary as to the degree of choice that they permit students regarding the field placement. Particularly in the foundation year of the MSW program or in the BSW program, students are sometimes assigned to a field placement or given a limited choice. It is common for one site to be recommended, with the option of refusal for student and field instructor after an interview.

A frequent concern arises for students when their interest in a certain population for a career choice is strong, and they are directed toward a totally different assignment for the foundation field placement. One young BSW student resisted the assignment to a Head Start program where she would be working with young parents and their pre-school age children, when her desire was to work with adolescents. She was concerned that this was not the type of job she would seek after graduation, and wondered if that would put her at a disadvantage at job hunting time. Her field coordinator assured her that: 1) the exposure to the social work role in this setting and the use of numerous social work skills would be very transferable (assessment, advocacy, brokering, linkage), 2) the experience of working with a seasoned field instructor who supported and challenged her students was invaluable, and finally, 3) the value of breadth of exposure to different populations and settings in the social work field is critical. The student decided to accept this, albeit with some reluctance.

How can the student, who does not have the benefit of hindsight, know how much confidence to put in this advice? Talking with other students, recent graduates, and more experienced professionals can help. When talking with graduates who are looking back on their educational experience, a very common comment heard is how highly they valued the diversity of exposure to different populations and settings that they had in their field internships. They stress the value in this upon reflecting on their own professional growth. Yet, this is less likely to be apparent to the student before the fact.

One student did reach this conclusion as he thought about his choices. For his undergrad placement, he was placed in an inpatient addictions program, which he liked very much but may have been a more specialized field than most undergrads are permitted. Upon graduating, he worked in the addictions field for a year, then entered the master's program. At first, he thought of keeping his job, and seeking permission to do an employer-based placement in the same agency. Fortunately, during class discussions, he began to realize how much he needed broader exposure to new client populations and different types of agency structures. He interviewed for and accepted a placement in a community action agency with multiple programs serving low-income families where, no doubt, he would use his experience with alcoholism in new and different ways.

Another example: For one student, the driving motivation was a desire to excel and an attraction to the appeal of clinical work—which would lead to an exciting and fulfilling social work career. This student indicated on a placement preference form that she wanted to be a psychotherapist, with a particular interest in diagnosing/treating clients with DSM-IV Axis II personality disorders. While possibly fine for this student after a number of years, looking at this student's approach to the placement selection process, it appeared that what the student thought was needed at the present and what the faculty thought was needed might be very different. This student needed time to experience herself in a variety of social work roles in a generalist practice context. It would be desirable for the student to get familiar with herself as a helping person in a lower stakes environment, given her newness to professional practice. Sometimes the field coordinator's role and/or the faculty advisor's role is that of preventing disaster by "nipping these kinds of mistakes in the bud." Thus, the student and the field coordinator/faculty advisor sometimes have different perspectives on what constitutes a "wise" choice of field placement.

Sometimes, a student may question a placement proposed by the field coordinator, because it is likely to immerse the student in value issues that seem daunting, even frightening. For example, the student who sees himself working with the elderly population and resists a placement with child protective services may be concerned about his ability to relate to the highly charged value issues abundant in child abuse cases. He may worry that his feelings about seeing children at risk, and his possible inability to protect them from further abuse, may arouse intense feelings that are more than he can handle. Many value issues may surface for students who are entering the field and feel real empathy for certain issues that may resonate with them personally, but who are reluctant to touch other issues that social workers deal with. Quite frequently, students who confront new populations with whom they have had no prior exposure and work through their own feelings of discomfort within the context of a supportive professional internship find themselves emerging with a new appreciation for the core social work principles and values.

Regardless of whether your social work program gives limited choice or wide latitude in making the field placement decision, you need to be able to ask questions comfortably, raising your doubts and concerns about field placement choices and assignments. Upon sharing and seeking feedback, students need to sort out their career interests, their personal strengths, and limitations to accomplish a good "fit" (that word that we started with!). They need to deal with the choices they have pro-actively and sensitively, while hearing the judgment and experience of the faculty and field instructor. Thus, the decision needs to be an open one with multiple participants. Field coordinators and faculty advisors or liaisons can help you with these decisions.

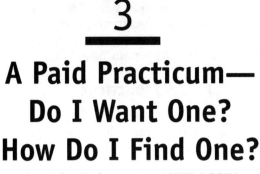

3

A Paid Practicum—
Do I Want One?
How Do I Find One?

by Julie Birkenmaier, MSW, LCSW

With increasing tuition costs, many social work students find themselves juggling practicum requirements with other obligations—work, classes, family, and life commitments. Some students find that they must mold the practicum around their other responsibilities, rather than enjoy an opportunity to focus their energies on this career-building experience. A paid practicum may help a student alleviate some of this pressure by combining practicum with a means of financial support. There are many issues to consider in the decision to pursue and accept a paid practicum.

Paid Practicum Policy

In an effort to accommodate the need for income while in school, social work programs can create and maintain paid practicum opportunities for students. Although the Council on Social Work Education (CSWE) has extensive guidelines for practica and has developed specific guidelines for practica completed by students employed at the practicum agency (Council on Social Work Education, 1994), no additional guidelines are in place for practica for which compensation is provided.

Social work programs vary widely in their policies and procedures governing the field education component of the curriculum. For instance, some programs assign practicum sites with little student input, while others allow for complete student self-selection. For those students interested in a paid practicum and able to provide significant input into their practicum site selection, information about the role of money in the field placement process is crucial to the decision-making process. What are the advantages and disadvantages of completing a paid practicum?

Advantages of a Paid Practicum

While considering the pursuit of a paid practicum, several distinct advantages emerge, including:

1. *Ease of financial burden and stress*—Combining practicum with a source of income allows one to focus energies on learning while paying bills. Students who must work at "outside" jobs often find their attention and energies divided as they struggle to make ends meet, complete their schooling, and meet other life commitments.

2. *Investment/connection to agency*—The role of intern can often be ambiguous, often existing in the "netherworld" between employee and volunteer. Receiving payment for a practicum may assist in clarifying the role and responsibilities of the intern to all concerned. The student may feel more of a sense of connection and commitment to the agency in exchange for payment.

3. *Possible stepping stone to paid employment*—Many agencies consider paid students to be employees. If the student meets or exceeds the supervisor's expectations during the practicum, the student may enjoy an advantage over other applicants for an opening at the agency.

4. *Paid experience weighted more heavily*—Paid experience can be given more consideration than volunteer work in the job-seeking process. A reference from a paid practicum experience may be considered equal in weight to a reference from a paid social work job.

Disadvantages of a Paid Practicum

While the advantages of a paid practicum may be clear, the disadvantages must be considered before a decision may be reached. Disadvantages for the student may include:

1. *Deterrent from learning goals*—For a financially strapped student, the lure of a paid practicum has the potential to dissuade even the best laid plans for the practicum. Students sometimes find that they must set their immediate career-building interests aside to accept a practicum that offers payment.

2. *Constraints on the opportunity to critically analyze aspects of agency functioning*—The paid practicum student may feel inhibited from offering constructive criticism of aspects of the experience that impact learning goals (i.e., supervision, administrative structure and process, policies) because they are considered more of an employee than a student.

3. *Extra requirements*—While some unpaid practicum opportunities may involve lengthy procedures prior to acceptance, many students find that securing the paid opportunity frequently involves lengthy procedures. Students may find that multiple interviews are required, while the norm for an unpaid practicum is only one interview. Furthermore, administrative approval to accept the student may be required, while approval from the proposed field instructor is the norm for unpaid practica. Other requirements for a paid practicum could include successful completion and approval of an application, a criminal background check, reference checks, and a drug and/or health screening. Some students find that paid sites require more hours or a longer-term commitment than specified by their school for practicum. Students may find it necessary to complete activities and tasks for the agency or organization after the practicum requirements for the school have been met.

4. *Role confusion and conflict*—Students receiving payment for practicum activities may feel compelled or may be encouraged to assist the agency in any way needed without regard to the completion of learning objectives. Agency staff and volunteers may view the paid student as "staff," thereby assuming that the student should show unreasonable flexibility in work/practicum activi-

ties. Students could find themselves substantially involved in work unrelated to learning objectives (i.e., clerical work or janitorial work) or only offered a very limited variety of tasks. Without a specified set of learning objectives and tasks specified by the school and agreed to by all concerned, learning could be compromised.

The potential for conflict between employment and school tasks and expectations has prompted some schools to develop a variety of contracting and monitoring policies with the aim of enhancing the student status as a student and not an employee (Martin, 1991). Martin further reports that only 10% of social work programs view practicum at place of employment as "very positive," while 59% assess the arrangement as "not very positive." These findings may be indicative of the problems that can occur when completing a practicum and generating income at the same site.

Possible Sources of Funds for a Paid Practicum

Social work programs may elect to prohibit student compensation for practicum activities. However, for those students attending schools that allow paid placements, there is a wide variety of possible sources for funding to explore. Among the funding sources for a paid practicum are:

1. *Government funding*—A variety of government funding options can be made available for stipends. Most Veterans Administration hospitals across the country offer training programs with the possibility of a paid practicum for second-year graduate students. Additionally, many baccalaureate and master's level social work education programs use federal Title IV-E funding to financially support students working within the public child welfare system (Zlotnik, 1997). Some states elect to support social work training in public schools through the availability of stipend funds for students. The AmeriCorps and Vista programs have been successfully utilized as sources of paid practica. Other state and local agencies may elect to use discretionary funds, such as "consulting fees," to pay students.

2. *Place of employment practica*—For students employed in social service-related settings, completing practica with their employers is an option in some programs. In a recent survey of MSW programs, over 9% of students enrolled have used employment sites as a practicum setting with the range being 0-27% (Martin, 1991). In some cases, students have negotiated with their employers to complete some or all practicum activities on work time while they are "on the payroll." While some social work programs restrict place of employment practica, many have developed special policies, and some schools have developed special programs for employed students who elect to remain at their work settings (Martin, 1991).

3. *Filling in for staff member on leave*—When agency staff take a sabbatical or leave to care for a new child or a sick relative, a need is created for a "temporary worker" in the agency. Depending on the level of knowledge and skill needed for the job duties, a paid practicum may be a positive alternative for the student, the employee, and the agency.

4 *University-secured funding*—Some social work programs have developed paid sites through a variety of university-generated sources. These sources can include: a) foundation support or grants, b) research funds used to create paid research assistantships, and/or c) funds from an endowment to support social work practice with a particular emphasis.

5. *Agency-based grants and funds*—Some agencies have included stipend funds for practica in grant proposal budgets. Other agencies have allocated stipend funds for students in their annual budgets. If the agency relies on student labor to fulfill specific duties and would like to have students each semester, offering a stipend can be a very effective incentive in recruiting students.

6. *Secure a new job*—If a new job is at a practicum site and entails new and appropriate learning for the student, some social work programs will allow a student to complete a placement within this arrangement.

Compensation for practicum activities can take many forms. Payment may be based on an hourly wage or a pre-determined stipend paid in bi-weekly, monthly, or lump sum payments for the semester. University-funded paid practica may involve tuition assistance. For those students in a practicum at a place of employment who are able to negotiate the completion of practicum activities on work time, payment could be considered the continuation of a regular paycheck. A practicum site that is unable to compensate a student for all practicum activities may be able to offer a stipend for specific activities that are under the purview of a grant or contract.

Tips for Securing a Paid Practicum

You have debated the pros and cons and are interested in pursuing a paid practicum. If you are attending a school that permits, facilitates, and supports this arrangement, securing a practicum that pays will take planning and preparation. The process of locating a paid practicum is often very similar to the job-seeking process.

Factors that will contribute to securing a paid practicum include prior social work experience (paid or unpaid), a proven academic track record, good networking skills, flexibility, creativity, determination, negotiation skills, timing, and sheer luck. Many agencies and organizations that have funds for stipends or payment will only "hire" a student for a paid practicum if the student also fits the criteria they have crafted for an employee.

If you are seeking a paid practicum, consider the following:

1. *Start the process early.* Become familiar with the procedures and policies guiding practica in your social work program. Complete the necessary paperwork and meet with your faculty liaison as soon as possible to explore possibilities. Paid practicum opportunities often are the first to be filled.

2. *Utilize your practicum liaison.* Your designated practicum liaison is there to assist in all phases of the practicum. The liaison is an important source of information about sites and can assist in the development of a new

or renewing paid practicum site. You can expect your practicum liaison to offer appropriate challenge and support in your decision-making process. Approach your liaison with your ideas for new paid practicum sites. Stay in close contact with your liaison throughout the planning semester to monitor for new paid practicum options that emerge.

3. *Network with faculty, students, alumni, and other social workers.* Use all your social work-related contacts to learn about paid opportunities and to communicate your interests.

4. *Polish your résumé and interviewing skills.* Update your résumé and ask others to review it. Practice your interviewing skills with friends and family. Remember that many agencies will only hire a student for practicum if the student also fits the criteria for an employee.

5. *Monitor employment ads.* If a new job would entail new appropriate learning, you may be able to complete practicum requirements simultaneously with employment duties or negotiate a practicum at your new place of employment.

The Final Decision

Before accepting an offer of a paid practicum, ponder the possibilities. Ask yourself the following questions:

1. Does this practicum opportunity entail significant, new, and appropriate learning for me?

2. Does this practicum opportunity include the skills and experiences that I am seeking at this point in my social work program?

3. Does this practicum opportunity appear to offer the experiences that will lead me toward my long-term career goals?

4. Would I accept this practicum if payment was not an
    option?

5. If desired by the agency, am I willing to complete tasks
    and activities beyond the requirements of the social work
    program?

    If you answer "no" to a significant number of these ques-
tions, you may well need to reconsider the offer. Ask yourself, "Is the financial gain worth the sacrifice of my present
educational goals?"

Conclusion

    The practicum experience is often pivotal in shaping ca-
reer interests and directions. A paid practicum that entails
new appropriate learning in the direction of the career interests of the student can be advantageous for all involved.
Knowing where the pitfalls may lie can be helpful in avoiding potential conflicts.

References

Council on Social Work Education (1994). *Handbook of accreditation standards and procedures* (4th edition). Alexandria, VA: Author.

Martin, M. L. (1991). Employment setting as practicum site:
A field instruction dilemma. In D. Schneck, B. Grossman, &
U. Glassman, *Field education in social work. Contemporary
issues and trends* (pp. 288-294). Dubuque, IA: Kendall/
Hunt.

Zlotnik, J. L. (1997). Survey findings on use of Title IV-E
training funds. *Social Work Education Reporter, 45* (1), 8-11.

*Special thanks go to Eugene Kain (United States Pretrial Ser-
vices), Don Moses (United States Veterans Administration),
and Marla Berg-Weger, Ph.D. (Saint Louis University School
of Social Service) for information that contributed to this chapter.*

4

Can I Do My Practicum Where I Work?

by Marla Berg-Weger, Ph.D., LCSW, and
Pamela J. Huggins, LCSW

You have just had a brainstorm—why not do your next practicum at your job? You begin to formulate a rationale in your mind: 1) you are already working in social services, 2) you could make a contribution to the agency, and 3) life would be much less complicated if you did not have to locate and complete a practicum in addition to your job. Now, the next step is to find out if such a plan is an option at your school. You have heard on the student grapevine that some students have sought and received approval for this, but you have no idea how to negotiate the system.

Practica at place of employment present a challenge for students, schools of social work, and the Council on Social Work Education (CSWE). CSWE, in the most recent *Handbook of Accreditation Standards and Procedures* (1994), provides general guidelines for practica completed by students employed at the practicum agency, but allows individual social work programs to implement procedures for approving and monitoring these practicum arrangements. CSWE specifies the following: 1) student should be assured of adequate release time for course and field work, 2) practicum activities should be distinguished from employment activities, 3) curricular and practicum requirements should not differ for students in these situations, and 4) practicum activities should emphasize educational goals (versus service to the agency) (CSWE, 1994).

Utilizing these guidelines, schools of social work have developed a variety of mechanisms for responding to the increasing need for practica to be completed at the student's place of employment. Martin (1991) cites reasons for increased requests as: increasing tuition costs coupled with decreasing student financial aid, continuity for the agency and the student, and increasing numbers of students entering schools of social work while being employed in social service agencies. Further, enabling a student to complete a portion or all of the practicum requirement at his/her place of employment may serve as a recruitment strategy for schools of social work in times of competition for student applicant market share.

In a survey of sixty-three MSW programs, directors of field education reported that approximately 9% of students complete practicum at their place of employment with the range being 0-27% (Martin, 1991). This survey also yielded data to suggest that large and medium schools (250-550 and 150-250 students, respectively) report 10-20% of students complete practica at their place of employment, while smaller schools (less than 150 students) have a range from 5-25% of students who complete practica at their employment site (Martin, 1991). There is considerable variation among schools from those that do not permit practicum at place of employment to those that have developed specialized programs for students employed as social workers. However, most schools have developed criteria for students who request this type of practicum experience. While these criteria differ in implementation, there are similarities across the schools in terms of scope and focus of the criteria.

Advantages of Practicum at Place of Employment

You continue to contemplate the possibility of a practicum at your place of employment. While this arrangement would simplify your hectic life, you ask yourself if there are educational, professional, and personal advantages to completing a practicum at your job site.

For the student, advantages of completing a practicum at one's place of employment may be considerable. They include:

1. *Flexibility*—Students find that the option to complete practicum hours during the work day as well as evening and weekends enables them to balance busy lives.

2. *Service to the agency* —Student practica at place of employment can fulfill agency needs that may often go unmet because of diminishing staff and resources. This type of practicum arrangement can provide an opportunity for a student who is already familiar with the organization to adeptly meet the need while optimizing the student's educational experience.

3. *Opportunity to learn different aspects of the agency/organization*—Students benefit from experiencing the broader range of agency services, as well as being challenged by "new" learning. Often, students may have worked in only one area of an agency, and a practicum can expand student knowledge and understanding of the agency's overall functioning and the interrelationships between agency departments and the agency and the community.

4. *Opportunity to prepare for a higher level position*—With expanded roles within the agency, students completing practica at one's place of employment become qualified for leadership positions within the agency. A practicum may provide agency administration with a new and more diverse perspective on the student and his or her capabilities.

5. *Potential opportunities for tuition support and/or cost-sharing arrangements with the school*— Many agencies that are motivated to upgrade employees' skills are willing to offer cost-sharing of tuition for a committed employee who will then continue to serve the agency in an expanded capacity.

6. *Financial "relief" for the student*—Students completing practica at their place of employment may not have to sacrifice their source of income in order to fulfill practicum requirements. In addition to maintaining part- or full-time employment, the agency may be able and/or willing to compensate the student for a portion of the work hours devoted to practicum. This option can provide students with a decreased sense of emotional and financial burden.

Practica at the student's place of employment can result in rewards for all parties involved—student, agency and the school of social work. Schools of social work are becoming more responsive to community agency needs while being creative in having educational objectives met. Agencies may relish the opportunity to have their own employees complete a long awaited project. Many students seeking additional education are working in social services. With diminished social service funding and financial support for higher education, schools must design practica programs that address the realities of the day.

Disadvantages of Practicum at Place of Employment

Just as you have considered the benefits of practicum at your place of employment, you begin to wonder if there are disadvantages of such an arrangement.

While there may be potential gains from completing a practicum at one's place of employment, disadvantages must be considered before reaching a decision. Disadvantages for the student may include:

1. *Quality of learning experience*—Because students enter this practicum experience with an extensive knowledge and familiarity with the agency, the practicum may not provide a high level or quality of new learning.

2. *Monitoring*—Because of the relationships students may have formed with agency personnel, the practicum experience may not be as closely monitored by field instructors, as they may perceive the student as being capable of functioning in this new role based on previous experience with the student as a co-worker.

3. *Dual identities and relationships*—The role of student and employee may become blurred for the student, other employees, employer(s), and field instructor. Students may find themselves in awkward positions if the agency views them as an employee first and a learner second. Additionally, students may not adequately seek super-

vision as they do not wish to compromise their role as an employee.

4. *Agency demands*—Unintentionally, the agency may take advantage of these students in an effort to meet ever increasing service demands. This may result in a lack of protected time and supervision required for the practicum. Students can experience difficulty negotiating their learning experience when these roles compete and conflict.

Just as there are disadvantages from the student's perspective regarding practicum at place of employment, schools of social work have some reticence about promoting these type of practica, as well. Martin (1991) reports that only 10% of schools of social work viewed these experiences as "very positive," while 59% perceive the experience to be "not very positive" and 19% find the experience to be "not positive at all." Schools of social work share students' concerns regarding practica at the place of employment, particularly in the areas of new and quality learning, monitoring, and student role confusion and conflict.

Structure and Process for Successful Practica at Place of Employment

You have weighed the options and have decided to pursue completing a practicum at your place of employment. What are the steps and criteria involved?

As noted, the majority of schools of social work do offer students the option to complete a portion of the practicum requirement at the student's current place of employment. Despite different interpretations of the CSWE guidelines regarding these practica, there are common elements that exist throughout the procedures (Martin, 1991). Some schools specify the number of practica that can be completed at the student's place of employment, the point in the student's educational plan that this type of practica may be implemented, and the student's status within the agency. These general criteria may be summarized as listed below:

1. Agency must meet school's criteria for approval as a practicum site.

2. Practicum-related tasks and activities must be entirely different from the student's usual employment duties. For optimal learning, the student may choose to complete practica in a different area of the agency from the one in which he or she is employed (department, unit, site).

3. Practicum-related tasks and activities cannot be equivalent to a full-time employee workload.

4. The student's employment supervisor cannot serve as the field instructor for the practicum (Martin, 1991).

Schools of social work strive to foster quality training in the field. At the same time, schools work to accommodate student needs and lifestyles. Developing clear and comprehensive criteria for completing practica at the student's place of employment is an attempt by schools of social work to protect the educational goals and objectives for the student's learning experience, since they have sought a baccalaureate or master's social work degree.

At the authors' program at Saint Louis University School of Social Service, the faculty have become aware of an increasing number of students who are employed in full-time positions in social services while maintaining a part- or full-time courseload in the social work program. In an effort to address the practicum needs of this student population, we have developed specific criteria for MSW students who request approval to complete practica at their place of employment (BSW students do not traditionally complete practica at place of employment). These criteria build on the CSWE guidelines and are similar to those reported by other schools of social work.

Upon determining that he or she would like to pursue a practicum at the place of employment, the student meets with the faculty liaison to discuss the educational merits of such an arrangement. Specifically, the liaison addresses with the student such issues as: opportunities for new learning that are at a higher level and commensurate with the BSW or MSW roles and responsibilities, supervision and the compatibility of agency needs, and goals of the school and the student. Students may complete the first portion of the required practicum hours at their place of employment, as the School feels strongly that the student should experience the delivery of social services in a variety of settings for optimal educational fulfillment.

In conjunction with agency personnel, the student develops a written proposal for completing practicum at his or her place of employment. This proposal includes: description of current social work duties, plan for practicum tasks and activities, work and practicum schedules, and supervision arrangement. The proposal must be endorsed by the student, employment supervisor, field instructor, faculty liaison, academic advisor, and director of practicum.

Liaison Role: Monitoring and Evaluation

You have been approved to complete your next practicum at your place of employment. You are wondering what the school's role will be and how concerns or problems will be addressed.

While most schools do not develop separate criteria for monitoring practica at students' places of employment, other schools require additional visits and/or learning contracts (Martin, 1991). The student's school of social work will provide support for developing appropriate learning tasks and activities at the site. The designated practicum liaison serves as a key resource for this experience. The school's liaison may assist all parties, defining appropriate roles and learning experiences for the practicum, monitoring the progress, and participating in the evaluation. The practicum liaison pays particular attention to the issues of dual roles, conflict, and exploitation and may need to assist the student and agency in re-negotiating the practicum structure.

To Do or Not To Do . . .?

You have reviewed all the pros and cons of completing a practicum at your place of employment. You are now equipped with the tools to determine if this experience is right for you. You recognize that this practicum arrangement may be a valuable and efficient strategy for completing your professional social work education. Now, the question becomes...to do or not to do?

References

Council on Social Work Education. (1994). *Handbook of Accreditation Standards and Procedures (Fourth Edition)*. Alexandria, VA: Author.

Martin, M.L. (1991). Employment setting as practicum site: A field instruction dilemma. In D. Schneck, B. Grossman, & U. Glassman, *Field education in social work. Contemporary issues and trends* (pp. 288-294). Dubuque, Iowa: Kendall/ Hunt.

PART II

GETTING READY

PART II: GETTING READY

You have your field placement assignment, and you're excited about getting "out in the real world." The first day of placement is around the corner.

What is expected of you? What are you expecting of yourself? Are you ready?

Your learning plan will help you determine and measure those expectations. It is a useful tool that will serve you well. Think about what you want to accomplish and how you will know when you have accomplished it. You may find that your goals change as you move through your practicum. If so, that's okay. The learning plan is a starting point. You may experience some variations along the way, but it will help you reach your destination.

The field liaison at your school is another helpful resource. This is the person who serves as a "bridge" between the agency and the school. Develop a good relationship with the liaison; he or she can help you through both the smooth and the rough spots.

You may wonder what a chapter on writing skills is doing in this section. You're not an English major, after all. Actually, writing is one of the most important communication tools you have at your disposal as a future social worker. Besides being able to listen attentively and communicate effectively with verbal language, you will need to convey information to other professionals through your progress notes and other client records. Eventually, you may want to share your knowledge with other professionals by writing a journal article. As a professional, you must be able to write in a way that will convey your thoughts, observations, and concrete information in a meaningful way.

What other tools do you have at your fingertips? Get your toolbox organized, and you'll be all set to go.

5

Listen Up!

by Betsy C. Mistek, BSSW

So, you've finally made it to the point of your practicum. You've completed, or soon will complete, your senior paper or thesis, that painful yet worthwhile experience. (You might not think that now, but later on you will!) You think you will never experience stress like that, and you can handle anything now. Sound familiar? That's how I felt last semester. I was VERY stressed out having to work on my senior paper *and* do all the other coursework for other classes. It is a lot to do, but I'm glad I went through it when I did. I felt I could handle ANYTHING!

But I was only beginning to experience stress. I started my senior practicum this fall in an elementary school. I have to drive an hour and 15 minutes Tuesdays through Fridays to be at my site by 7:30 a.m. That means I am up by 4:45 a.m. and leave my house by 6:15 a.m. I have to make sure my clothes are ironed and figure out a professional outfit to wear for the day, without having to look like a "college student." I usually don't get to leave my agency until 4:30-5:00 p.m. Yeah, I could leave earlier and only put in my eight hours for the day, but I want to make a good impression on my supervisor, and I don't want to miss out on important meetings. Trust me, putting in these extra hours pays off in more ways than one.

So, I don't get home until 6:30 at the earliest on any given night. On Tuesdays, I go straight to work for a couple of hours, so I have at least *some* money to my name. The other nights I spend doing research, reading, and writing papers for Practice III and Seminar. It's not easy trying to get all of that done, get to bed at a decent hour, and be able to get up at 4:45 every morning. Plus, because I want to make my practicum experience as worthwhile as I possibly can, I read articles and books given to me by my supervisor, who wants to make me as knowledgeable as she can. She is extending her resources and making my practicum a great learning experience. I can't pass up this opportunity to read about something that I will be experiencing soon.

My weekends are spent catching up on homework, laundry, bills, cleaning house, spending time with friends and family, and trying to work more to make some more money. At the same time, I am planning on moving to another city. I need to find a job and a place to live. That's not easy to do from four hours away. Thank GOD for the INTERNET! Searching for the right job, or the right place to live, consumes a lot of my time.

Also, I am planning on graduating, so I need to make sure I get what I need to walk at the ceremony. That takes up the two hours between classes that I have to spare on Mondays, the only days I'm on campus.

So far, it just appears as though time management and organization are my only stresses, right? Wrong. I haven't even gotten to dealing with the "real world" experience that the practicum gives you. I run my own groups, meet with kids on an individual basis, help kids work through their problems, interview parents and students, and consult with teachers. I run out to a kid's house to see why he's not in school, write up assessment reports, meet with other professionals to discuss the needs of kids, and attend meetings in the community. I come up with games and topics for my groups, make copies, assist my supervisor in her classroom instruction on conflict resolution and peer mediation, and answer phone calls from upset parents. I observe students in the classroom, during lunch, and during recess. These are only a few things that I have experienced. I leave that school at night and wonder about the kids I see. I worry about them. I worry about the report I wrote up. I worry about confidentiality. What do I say? When do I say it? How should I say it? To whom can I say it? What about other ethical issues? I feel as though these kids' lives are in my hands. There is so much I want to do, but not enough time.

What about those days when I spend the whole day running around trying to solve all these problems and never get a break to eat lunch? What about the days when there just seems to be a never-ending line of kids who need our services, or a teacher who needs us to meet with a student who is having some problems? What about the days I leave almost in tears feeling helpless that there's only so much I can do for the kids, and the rest being up to them? I'm only a student—I'm not here on a long-term basis. I need to figure out a way to say good-bye and have closure on the situation. Now I need to worry about these kids after I leave. It's not that I don't trust my supervisor to do a wonderful job, because I know she will. I am just worried that the two of us were doing the job of at least two or three people. And now she's the only one.

I thought that after last semester, I could handle anything. Anything academic, that is. Academic stress is a little different from real-life stress. After writing a 30+-page paper, I can easily handle a 6- to 10-page paper—NO PROBLEM! But having to deal with the worry of my practicum experience, putting in long days, feeling limited in what I know and what I can do, and having to worry about all the other baggage that we all carry with us in our personal lives— it isn't easy, folks.

Don't go into your practicum thinking it will be a breeze. It's not. Academically, yes it is easier. The stress is just different. You're graduating, looking for a job, possibly thinking about moving and finding a different place to live, preparing for the state licensure exam, the merit exam, finding time to take those exams, worrying about how you are doing in your agency, and worrying about making this the most beneficial experience of your college career.

I don't want to make any of this sound negative, because my practicum experience has been a most positive one. I have learned so much about myself, my knowledge, the application of that knowledge, my capabilities as a social worker, and the role of the social worker in an agency. I have a wonderful supervisor who has taught me great things and has taken me under her wing and shown me the way. The amount of gratitude I owe her cannot be measured. The things she has taught me, I can't learn in a classroom. I have put so much effort into my experience, and thus, I am getting so much more out of it.

So, what am I saying? Be prepared for anything. Be flexible. Be professional. And most of all, be true to yourself. Make your practicum experience the best you can. This is your chance to try all those things you've learned in school. Take advantage of all the opportunities that come your way. Be sure to communicate with your supervisor and professors. They are your advocates! Let them know how things are going, and if you need help. They are there to help you. Utilize that resource! I wish you all the best of luck.

6

10 Tips for a Successful Field Placement

by Jan Ligon, Ph.D., LCSW, and
Jim Ward, MSW

Entering the field practicum is an exciting and important event for social work students. As a new experience, it is normal for some students to experience some degree of anxiety about the placement. As new relationships begin with your agency field instructor and your faculty liaison, it is important to clarify your role as a student. These suggestions are offered as a helpful guide as you move into your field experience.

1. Read the field manual or booklet provided by your program. It is important to become familiar with the many details and procedures associated with your field practicum.

2. Read the NASW *Code of Ethics* and become familiar with its contents. Students should pay particular attention to Section 1.03, Informed Consent; Section 1.04, Competence; and Section 3.02, Education and Training.

3. Ask questions about information concerning the field manual or the *Code of Ethics* that may be confusing or unclear. Although reading the materials is an important first step, you will also want to learn when and how to use your field instructor and other social workers as resources to help answer questions or deal with issues that may not be adequately explained or covered by the content in your field manual, the *Code of Ethics,* or other documents.

4. Begin your placement with an adequate orientation of your agency. The orientation should include any policies, procedures, or forms that you will need to know about during your internship.

5. Take your learning plan or contract seriously. Make time to discuss what you want to learn and accomplish during your placement, and then jointly write a clear and realistic learning plan with your field instructor and faculty liaison. It is essential that your learning objectives are written at the proper educational level; conversely, they should not be set at levels that are either above or below that of your program. A review of Bloom's taxonomy of learning objectives (Pregent, 1994) may be helpful in finalizing learning objectives.

6. Address personal safety issues at your agency. Be sure that you are comfortable with all safety matters and with any emergency procedures that are relevant. These procedures may include evacuation plans in case of fire or other emergencies, personal safety in your agency, and safety procedures concerning such matters as parking or storage of personal valuables. Griffin (1995) provides a helpful overview of agency safety issues including a *Staff Safety Risk Scale.*

7. Familiarize yourself with liability issues or risks that may need to be addressed. For example, the use of your personal automobile during your placement could be a liability for you that needs to be covered. A thorough understanding of agency procedures to assure client confidentiality, including records, is essential. Additional readings concerning malpractice and liability (Kurzman, 1995; Reamer, 1994) and legal issues (Zakutansky and Sirles, 1993) are available.

8. Schedule supervision appointments with your field instructor and field visits with your faculty liaison. Uninterrupted individual supervision is essential to your field learning experience, and scheduled appointments are the best assurance that you will get the time that you need for supervision. Also, it is important to structure your

supervision time around a planned written agenda to assure that essential issues are addressed during each session.

9. If you believe that you are not adequately prepared to provide a service or intervention, you should address the concern with your agency field instructor, so you can obtain any training or knowledge that is needed to be able to provide the service.

10. You need to be aware that many students may not have a "perfect" practicum experience. However, if you should experience significant problems, they should be discussed as soon as possible with your field instructor and faculty liaison.

Social workers often identify the field practicum experience as the single most important part of social work education. As the student, it is critical for you to do everything possible on your part to make your field experience a productive one. While our ten tips cannot include everything the student will need to know, they can help you get off to a good start as you begin this very exciting part of your social work education.

References

Griffin, W. V. (1995). Social worker and agency safety. In R. L. Edwards (Ed.), *Encyclopedia of social work* (19th ed., pp. 2293-2305), Washington, D.C.: NASW Press.

Kurzman, P. A. (1995). Professional liability and malpractice. In R. L. Edwards (Ed.), *Encyclopedia of social work* (19th ed., pp. 1921-1927), Washington, D.C.: NASW Press.

Reamer, F. G. (1994). *Social work malpractice and liability: Strategies for prevention.* New York: Columbia University Press.

Zakutansky, T. J., & Sirles, E. A. (1993). Ethical and legal issues in field education. *Journal of Social Work Education, 29,* 338-347.

7

The Learning Agreement: A Roadmap for Your Journey

Jan Ligon, PhD, LCSW
and Jim Ward, MSW

As you begin your field placement, it is important to pause for just a bit and look back on the events that led to your practicum location. Although the specific placement procedures vary greatly from program to program, it is likely that you expressed some interests that you have in social work. You may have visited more than one agency or more than one field instructor during the process. You were probably a bit nervous and likely didn't know exactly what to expect, and you still may have some uncertainties and many questions as you begin this very important part of your social work degree program. Like the rest of your program, your field experience will be a journey rather than an event, and unexpected things will happen along the way. For this reason, social work authors have noted that it can be helpful to have a map (Horejsi & Garthwait, 1999; Thomlison, Rogers, Collins, & Grinnell, 1996).

Like a map, the field learning agreement helps to lay out the course of your practicum experience in a way that is the most beneficial to you and that will get you there using the best route. Some programs refer to the document as a "learning plan," while others use the term "learning contract." However, Bogo and Vayda (1998) note that the term "contract" can have a legal meaning although these plans, in fact, are not legal documents. **Why** develop a learning plan? Royse, Dhooper, and Rompf (1999), note that a solid learning agreement can reduce misunderstandings, protect the student from being used as a "substitute employee" (p. 34), serve as a vehicle for allocating time, and provide a basis for accountability and progress.

Having noted **why** the learning agreement is important to you, let's move now to the basics of **who, what, when,** and **how** the document is developed. The **who** of this process is you as the student, your field instructor, and your field liaison. In many programs, the Director of Field Instruction for your program will ultimately review and approve the agreement. Keep in mind, as noted by Bogo and Vayda (1998), that as an adult learner, it is very important that you participate in this endeavor as a mutual process that includes input from you as well as those who will be involved in your practicum experience. Bogo and Vayda go on to note that a joint approach will lead to your "feeling more involved in the learning activity" (p. 63). **What** to include will vary by program; however, Horejsi and Garthwait (1999) note that your content is likely to include learning goals that cover three areas, beginning with *values* and how your personal beliefs and preferences can be incorporated with the professional values and ethics of the social work profession. Second, goals related to the development of *knowledge* during your practicum may include "terminology, facts, principles, concepts, and theories" (Horejsi & Garthwait, 1999, p. 21). Finally, goals will include *skills,* or the "techniques and procedures used by social workers" (p. 21) that you want to develop and refine during your internship.

In considering **when** to develop your learning plan, the general answer is at the start of your internship, so the full benefit of your contract can be realized. It is important to note, however, that it is very possible that your plan will require one or more changes during your placement. Let's look now at a step-by-step approach that covers the essentials of **how** to write the document:

Steps to Writing the Plan

1. As noted by Thomlison, et al. (1996), a review of the practicum planning form or other field curriculum guidelines can help you to "see exactly what it is that your social work program expects of you" (p. 102).

2. Familiarize yourself with the difference between *goals*, *objectives*, and *outcomes* (Horejsi & Garthwait, 1999; Rothman, 2000). *Goals* are broad, general statements about what you intend to learn. *Objectives* are specific steps that lead to the accomplishment of goals. *Outcomes* are the end results that are produced by your accomplishments that can be measured or observed. Berg-Weger and Birkenmaier (2000) note several methods of evaluation, including direct observation of you by your field instructor, review of your work (reports, tapes, and so forth), and the use of other tools such as process recordings or logs.

3. Be aware of the **SPIRO** approach to developing goals (Royse, Dhooper, & Rompf, 1999). **SPIRO** posits that a goal should be **S**pecific (not global), **P**erformance-oriented (includes activities), spells out your **I**nvolvement in accomplishing the goal, is **R**ealistic (can be accomplished during your practicum), and **O**bservable (based on behavior or products that can be measured).

4. Partialize your objectives into bite-size pieces. Your objectives should be written in increments that are manageable and doable.

5. Don't let your program's forms and policies drive out or exclude the inclusion of what you want to learn and accomplish from your practicum. Certainly, you will need to address the standards of your program, but that doesn't mean you have to do a "cookie cutter" learning plan that isn't personalized to your needs and learning style.

6. Be creative. If you can't get what you need at your placement, is there a different approach that can address your need in another way? For example, we required that students have at least one experience with groups as a co-leader or facilitator during their practicum. If the agency didn't offer groups, the students would find other opportunities to accomplish this requirement with another agency or organization in the community.

Example

Cynthia's practicum is with a family services agency where she wants to focus on working with young children. Her program is stressing the need to learn about technology in conjunction with her placement, especially when it can be used to help clients, facilitate services, or evaluate outcomes of services. Cynthia feels a bit overwhelmed by this expectation, so her field instructor suggested the following goal for the learning plan she is developing:

Goal	Objective	Outcome—How Measure
To use technology to assist clients	Attend computer orientation	Validate attendance
	Complete psychosocial history using agency software	Psychosocial history completed

Cynthia didn't feel as if this helped very much. She didn't really know what was covered in the computer orientation session and she has previous experience from an earlier course in using technology to complete a social history. She then developed her own version, as shown on the next page.

Cynthia felt that the second goal and objectives seemed to fit better for several reasons. First, the goal addresses advancing client services; she wants to help children, and this goes beyond assistance. Second, the objectives are both realistic and targeted to her needs; after learning what technology is used by the agency, she can select one of these tools and actually use it with a client. The outcomes are very straightforward and move her closer to accomplishing the ultimate goal of learning how to use technology to enhance services. Also, the objectives and outcomes include dates, which adds accountability and insures forward movement. As these initial objectives are accomplished it is likely that new objectives will surface. For example, when she reviews her work, the field liaison might provide her with an additional resource that could be tried and might ultimately

Goal	Objective	Outcome—How Measure
To know how to use technology to advance client services	Document agency technology used in conjunction with client services by March 1st	Review brief written summary during supervision session by March 15th
	Use one technology tool with one client by March 20th	Evaluate use and document produced during supervision and with liaison for input by April 6th

be adopted by the agency. It is very common for students to bring new tools and ideas to their agencies, which ultimately can enhance services.

The learning plan can be a very helpful document for use in clarifying the expectations of the student; exploring both the assets and limitations of the agency; and for use in holding the student, liaison, and field instructor accountable. This doesn't mean that the plan must be lengthy; it's better to develop a plan that includes a modest number of goals that are really important and then develop measurable goals to lead to accomplishing each goal. Keep the language clear and straightforward.

Students are invariably anxious about grades, but the fact of the matter is that field instructors often feel exactly the same way! A solid learning plan greatly facilitates the process of evaluations at the end of the term and can ease those anxious feelings. Another way to reduce anxiety is to review your learning plan with both your field instructor and your liaison periodically. In fact, many liaisons will use the learning plan as a focus of discussion during field site visits. These check-ins can be very useful in identifying areas that are going well, as well as those that may need more attention.

Keep in mind that the document won't ever be perfect, and it can never cover everything. As noted by Horejsi and

Garthwait (1999), "don't be surprised if much of what you actually learn during your practicum was not anticipated and could not have been written into your plan" (p. 26). Indeed, your learning plan is like a map, but your practicum experience is more like a trip; you never know what to expect on a journey, but that's part of the excitement. Use your learning plan to help you gain as much from your internship experience as possible. It will serve you well later as you begin your career as a social worker.

References

Berg-Weger, M., & Birkenmaier, J. (2000). *The practicum companion for social work: Integrating class and field work.* Boston: Allyn and Bacon.

Bogo, M., & Vayda, E. (1998). *The practice of field instruction in social work: Theory and process.* New York: Columbia University Press.

Horejsi, C. R., & Garthwait, C. L. (1999). *The social work practicum: A guide and workbook for students.* Boston: Allyn and Bacon.

Rothman, J. C. (2000). *Stepping out into field: A field manual for social work students.* Boston: Allyn and Bacon.

Royse, D., Dhooper, S. S., & Rompf, E. L. (1999). *Field instruction: A guide for social work students.* New York: Longman.

Thomlison, B., Rogers, G., Collins, D., & Grinnell, R. M. (1996). *The social work practicum: An access guide.* Itasca, IL: Peacock.

8

10 Tips for Maximizing Your Field Liaison Relationship

by Jan Ligon, PhD, LCSW,
and Jim Ward, MSW

As your internship experience begins, you have already worked out many details about your placement with your Director of Field Instruction, met your Field Instructor, and begun courses that will be taken in conjunction with the field practicum. Another person who is very important to a successful field experience is the Field Liaison. All social work students are assigned a liaison to work with them throughout their internship experiences. The primary role of the liaison is to serve as the person who bridges or connects the relationships between you as the student, the field instructor, your Director of Field Instruction, and your social work program's curriculum. Your liaison, who may be affiliated with your college or university or a social worker from the community, will make visits to your field site each term and may also facilitate your field seminar. Although the liaison role has been noted as a critical one in social work education (Urbanowski & Dwyer, 1988), little has been written about the field liaison and its benefits to students (Bennett & Coe, 1998). Here are ten tips that you can use to maximize your liaison relationship and further enhance your internship experience.

1. ***Know the facts.***
    Consult your field manual and director to determine how the liaison fits into your field experience, how often site visits are made, how the liaison's role fits into developing and evaluating your learning plan outcomes, and how you can contact your liaison. Find out about your liaison's interests and experience in social work.

2. *Make an appointment.*
   Contact your liaison and arrange for a convenient time to meet. During your session, let your liaison know about your career interests in social work, your previous volunteer and work experiences, and your learning objectives for your practicum.

3. *Get the lowdown.*
   Find out how the liaison views the field placement and get a feel for overall expectations, including sensitivities. For example, some liaisons may be very concerned about how students will dress on field days, while this might not be a concern at all for others. Everyone is different.

4. *Learn the ropes.*
   As noted by Faria, Brownstein, & Smith (1988), liaisons can serve students in a number of roles, including mediator, monitor, consultant, advocate, and teacher. Although you may not personally experience all of these roles during your practicum, it is important to understand the breadth of the liaison role, that the role is a different entity than your field instructor's, and that your liaison is there to serve you in any of the above roles as needed.

5. *Make a plan.*
   As you develop your learning contract, be sure to solicit the input of your liaison so you are able to get the most from your placement. You will have already discussed your interests, and now is the time to focus on a plan of action.

6. *Avoid passivity.*
   You don't need to wait to hear from your liaison; send an occasional e-mail or check in by phone periodically during your placement. Remember that "consultant" is one of the roles noted by Faria et al. (1988), and you will want to take advantage of this aspect of your liaison relationship.

7. *Deal with problems.*
   Social workers are problem solvers, so it is important to

learn ways to resolve issues that may occur during your placement with your field instructor. Make particular note of student issues outlined in Section 3.02- Education and Training, in the NASW *Code of Ethics* (NASW, 1996) concerning competence, exploitation, and appropriate boundaries. If problems are not resolved, discuss them with your liaison, keeping in mind that your liaison is a different person who can share yet another perspective on any situation that may arise.

8. *Liaisons aren't just for problems.*
Students often seek out their liaison only about problems; however, this sets up the liaison as being the "complaint department" and can result in excluding the use of the liaison in such positive roles as teacher and consultant.

9. *Be practical.*
Remember that social workers practice in a very close knit profession. It is important to develop good working relationships with those in the social work community, including your practicum. In the short term, you may want to ask your liaison or field instructor for a reference; longer term, you could very likely become the field instructor who works with the liaison and a future student. You won't always be a student!

10. *Give feedback.*
As a student, you are accustomed to feedback on exams, papers, and field visits. Liaisons are people, too, and can benefit from not only your suggestions on what might be more helpful to you in the future, but also your input on what you found to be particularly beneficial in your relationship with your liaison.

Example

Jennifer, who was completing the first part of her practicum at a child welfare agency, met with her field instructor to review her evaluation. The field instructor gave her low ratings in three areas, which Jennifer felt was very unfair, since she had been given little direction in these particular aspects of the internship. Jennifer shared the situation with another student, including the fact that she didn't express her feelings further during the meeting. Her friend suggested that she contact her field liaison to discuss what had happened. Jennifer told her friend that she wasn't sure if that would help, as she perceived the liaison and the field instructor as "sort of a team," but then decided that maybe it was worth a try (see #4).

Her liaison contacted the field instructor to arrange for a meeting with Jennifer, the liaison, and the field instructor. They met and, together, reviewed the learning plan and revised it for the next term to clarify the areas of disagreement, and also to reinforce areas where Jennifer had shown significant growth (see #4 and #5). The meeting went well, and Jennifer felt much better about the overall situation, and she was glad that it all worked out it a positive way (see #9). She shared with the liaison how helpful the meeting had been (see #10). She also pledged to make more frequent contact with her liaison during the next term and to assert herself more during supervision sessions with her field instructor (see # 6).

What suggestions do you think the liaison had for Jennifer? First, the supervision time with her field instructor needed to include check-ins with the learning plan throughout the practicum (see #2 and #5). Second, it was important for Jennifer to follow through on her commitment to work on having open discussions with her field instructor and to obtain constructive feedback on her progress (see #6). Third, through this experience, she could more fully understand that there were many ways that her liaison could be a valuable resource throughout her internship experience (see # 4 and #8).

Your field liaison can play a vital role in helping you to get the most from your field experience. Fortune, et al. (1985) found that students who have access and frequent contacts with their liaisons are the most satisfied with their liaison relationships. Although the literal definition of liaison is associated with linking, in social work education your liaison can be your bridge to both your field placement and your social work program. Take full advantage of this valuable resource!

References

Bennett, L. & Coe, S. (1998). Social work field instructor satisfaction with faculty field liaisons. *Journal of Social Work Education, 34,* 345-352.

National Association of Social Workers. (1996). Code of ethics of the National Association of Social Workers. Washington, D.C.: Author.

Faria, G., Brownstein, C., & Smith, H. Y. (1988). A survey of field instructor's perceptions of the liaison role. *Journal of Social Work Education, 24,* 135-144.

Fortune, A. E., Feathers, C. E., Rook, S. R., Scrimenti, R. M., Smollen, P., Stemerman, B., & Tucker, E. L. (1985). Student satisfaction with field placement. *Journal of Social Work Education, 21,* 92-104.

Urbanowski, M., & Dwyer, M. M. (1988). *Learning through field instruction: A guide for teachers and students.* Milwaukee, WI: Family Service America.

9

Write On! Practical Suggestions for Preparing Social Work Records

by Katherine M. Dunlap, Ph.D., ACSW

Social workers are people-oriented. They enjoy meeting new clients, helping folks master problems, and watching clients and colleagues grow toward their full potential. Often, social workers do not like recording this process in case notes. "Let me work with people," my students frequently exclaim. "I want to make a difference, not write a novel!"

But the truth is that social workers often write documents that change people's lives. Court reports, grant proposals, and even case records can make dramatic differences in the circumstances of those we serve. To be good social workers, we must master not only the art of helping clients, but also the skill of writing about them and the services we provide. This chapter presents six simple strategies to help you improve your writing—and maybe even your attitude toward it.

First, make a time and place.

In our direct practice classes, we talk passionately about how to arrange chairs for an interview and how to ensure confidentiality, but we rarely mention the physical setting that helps us produce our reports. At a minimum, a writer needs a desk, adequate lighting, and paper and pens or a computer. Most need a quiet atmosphere to concentrate.

A little time and a quiet haven may be treasured commodities in a busy agency. Interns are likely to share telephones, desks, and cubicles with a supervisor or other student workers, and the noise levels in these areas can be quite high. Under these conditions, it is easy to relegate writing to second, third, or even fourth place. To avoid getting behind on reports, you must take charge of your time and place for writing.

- Structure your space to accommodate your writing.
- Clear your desk; give yourself room to work.
- Schedule a definite time for preparing daily reports, and stick to your schedule!
- Finish documents before you leave the office.
- Trade phone time with a colleague to reduce interruptions.
- Ask others to support your effort by keeping noise levels down.

Now that you have your basic tools and the proper setting, it's time to write! Here are a few more pointers to help you achieve success.

Second, assemble your tools.

Just as students need the *DSM-IV* (American Psychiatric Association, 1994) to complete a diagnosis, they need the proper resources to compile a professional document. To improve your writing, you will need four types of references: a dictionary, a thesaurus, a style manual, and a book that reviews the various types of social work notes. Each of these serves a different function.

The dictionary enables you to check spelling, exact meaning, and common usage of a word. If you are dictating notes, you must spell proper names and unusual words so the typist can prepare an accurate document. If you use word processing to write your own notes, learn to use the "spell-check" feature. But don't depend on this feature to correct all your errors; spelling checkers don't know whether you meant "their" or "there," for example.

The thesaurus helps you select the best word to describe a situation. For example, many words can express happiness: delighted, ecstatic, thrilled, glad, cheerful, merry. A thesaurus helps you paint a word picture that conveys your message with precision. *Bartlett's Roget's Thesaurus* (1996) is a standard reference book. Most word-processing programs now include an easy-to-use thesaurus.

A style manual is essential for research reports and papers while you are in school, and it will also be helpful after graduation. "This is my last paper," I often hear students say. "Wrong!" I muse. You may think that you will never write another paper after graduation, but you will probably find that you want to share your experiences with stakeholders, colleagues, and consumers. You may be asked to prepare an annual report, contribute to a grant proposal, or summarize the findings of a pilot program. You may see the need for consumer-friendly brochures, program descriptions, and agency manuals; you may want to present your experiences at an annual conference or share your thoughts in a journal. A style manual can help you with each of these writing projects.

Several style manuals are available. The most commonly used by social work journals is the *Publication Manual of the American Psychological Association*, often called the APA Manual (1994). Others include the *Chicago Manual of Style* (1993) and Turabian's classic text (1996). Before you buy a style manual, check to see if your school or employer has a preference.

The style manual shows the proper form for reference lists and bibliographies, and these are the sections you will use most often in school. But a style manual is much more than a guide for lists. It also provides information about typing, word usage, punctuation, and organization. For example, which is correct: "fifteen," "15," or "fifteen (15)"? How do you decide whether to use "farther" or "further"? Should you write "The Williams' " or "The Williamses"? Your style manual speaks to each of these and more.

In addition to these reference books, you will also need a book that describes different types of social work records. What is the difference between a process recording and a progress note? A psychosocial assessment and a social history? A SOAP note and a problem-oriented medical entry? A records manual specifies the form and content for each of these types of documentation. *Recording* by Wilson (1980) is a classic text that you are likely to see in your field instructor's bookcase. A more current choice might be *Social Work Records*, which provides a history of record-keeping, presents standard forms and formats, and discusses current issues in the field (Kagle, 1996).

These books are not expensive, and you can often find used editions in college bookstores. Try to purchase one each semester—be sure to get the latest edition—and soon, your armamentarium will be fully stocked!

Third, avoid gender-specific language.

Cardinal social work values include respect for the dignity and worth of the individual and the uniqueness of each person (Hepworth, Rooney, & Larsen, 1997; Compton & Galaway, 1994). In writing, we can operationalize these values by using non-gender-specific language (Dumond, 1990). In other words, we avoid phrases like "mankind" and "man-made." We eschew gender-specific words like "businessman," "policeman," and "congressman." Equally offensive are feminized words like "actress" and "waitress." Both your thesaurus and your style manual will suggest alternatives. For example, more accurate phrases such as "humankind" and "manufactured" can replace "mankind" and "man-made." For "businessman," "policeman," and "congressman," substitute "business executive," "police officer," and "member of Congress." Actor, server, and even waiter are accepted terms for both men and women in these roles. Finally, it is not necessary to state that a nurse is male or that a mechanic is female.

In professional writing, we don't refer to all clients collectively as either male or female. The easiest way to avoid using a global "he or she" is to make all pronouns plural. This leads to the next pointer.

Fourth, ensure noun/pronoun agreement.

In recent years, many conscientious writers have worked hard to avoid gender-specific language only to fall into another, equally awkward trap involving noun-pronoun agreement. For example:

When a social worker writes a court report, they should proofread it carefully.

The subject of this sentence, "social worker," is singular; but the pronoun, "they," is plural. This sentence can be fixed by bringing the pronoun into agreement with the noun; however, this leads us back to using either a gender-specific pronoun or the awkward and tiresome "he or she." A better solution is to make the noun plural. The sentence becomes:

When social workers write court reports, they should proofread them carefully.

Another solution is to rewrite the sentence and eliminate the pronoun entirely:

A social worker who writes a court report should proofread it carefully.

Fifth, practice proofreading.

Proofreading is an essential skill that can be learned. There are two methods of proofreading: by computer and the old-fashioned way—reading. Both techniques are valuable, and together, they help you create letter-perfect documents.

To proofread a computer-generated report, first use the spell-check feature. This device will catch commonly misspelled words. Second, use the grammar program to help you determine correct usage. Third, use word search to examine your particular challenges. For example, if you tend to have difficulty with noun/pronoun agreement, search for "their" and "they." Does each use follow a plural noun? Once you find your errors, you can easily rewrite your sentences.

While computer programs are helpful, they are not sufficient by themselves. They cannot discriminate among synonyms; and they do not catch correctly spelled substitutions such as "is" for "it," or "to" for "of." Even the best grammar program cannot help you achieve logical organization or comprehensive coverage. To master these details, writers must also learn to proofread their documents personally.

Start by looking at each word in each sentence. Concentrate first on the words themselves. Are they spelled correctly? Does each word precisely capture the essence of your message? Have you avoided gender-specific language and problems with agreement?

Second, look at content. Did you begin at the beginning? Did you state all essential facts? Did you cover the "Five Ws": who, what, when, where, and why? Did you include all essential elements for the type of report you are writing? Did you date and sign your note?

Third, have you organized your work so that it can be used easily by others? Each paragraph should have a beginning, middle, and end; and each report should contain the same elements. Categorical headings such as "client description," "goals," and "outcomes" help organize material, even if these are not included in the final version.

Sixth, write nothing more, nothing less.

Because social workers often write for other busy professionals, such as judges or physicians, our notes should concisely state pertinent facts without commenting on irrelevant issues. As E. B. White exhorts, "Omit needless words. Vigorous writing is concise" (1979, p. 23).

This dictum is also true in social work. Home health social workers need not address income or expenses unless financial concerns interfere with the patient's recovery. Home health progress notes should be limited to the specific conditions for which social work services have been ordered. Similarly, school social workers should not speculate on family issues they have not been asked to address, and eligibility specialists do not usually explore intrapsychic issues.

Unnecessary verbiage also creates a barrier to communication. When we stray from the presenting problem, insert personal opinions, use pompous language, or ramble about superfluous details, the reader quickly loses interest, and the client loses out.

Here's one for practice.

The following note was written by a social worker at a service agency. Does this note contain all the facts needed for a decision about services? Does it include any extraneous material? Try your hand at identifying and correcting the variety of typographical errors, inconsistencies, and examples of poor writing in the following paragraph:

Mrs. Smith is an 64-year-old female living in Public Housing with her daughter, granddaughter, adult son. Ms. Smith come to Emergency Services to request assistence to purchasing food for her family. She reports that she has been the primary wage earner for this household, but was recently laid of from her job as a waitress. Mrs. Smith states that she has no savings as she has use everything too send her son to school to become a male nurse. Mrs. Smith cried when she tole me that her granddaughter had to accept free lunch. When the previous social worker interviewed her, they said she was not elegible for our services. Needs help.

Access campus resources.

At least 16 corrections are needed in the sample paragraph above. If you had difficulty identifying them, you may want to access the resources on your campus. Colleges and universities offer specific classes designed to develop technical writing skills. In addition, many schools offer workshops dealing with organization, writing anxiety, and time management. Peer tutoring and writing groups offer exciting, enjoyable opportunities to reinforce newly acquired skills.

Take advantage of campus services now. When you join the ranks of professional social workers, you will be richly rewarded for the time you invest today in writing.

References

American Psychiatric Association. (1994). *Diagnostic and statistical manual of mental disorders* (4th ed.). Washington, D.C.: Author.

American Psychological Association. (1994). *Publication manual of the American Psychological Association.* Washington, DC: Author.

Bartlett's Roget's Thesaurus. (1st ed.). (1996). Boston: Little, Brown, and Company.

Compton, B. R., & Galaway, B. (1994). *Social work processes* (5th ed.). Pacific Grove, CA: Brooks/Cole.

Dumond, V. (1990). *The elements of nonsexist usage: A guide to inclusive spoken and written English.* New York: Prentice Hall.

Hepworth, D. H., Rooney, R. H., & Larsen, J. A. (1997). *Direct social work practice: Theory and skills* (5th ed.). Pacific Grove, CA: Brooks/Cole.

Kagle, J. D. (1996). *Social work records.* Prospect Heights, IL: Waveland Press.

Turabian, K. L. (1996). *A manual for writers of term papers, theses, and dissertations* (Rev. by J. Grossman & A. Bennett). (6th ed.). Chicago: University of Chicago Press.

University of Chicago Press. (1993). *The Chicago manual of style* (14th ed.). Chicago: Author.

White, E. B. (1979). *Elements of style* (3rd ed.). New York: MacMillan.

Wilson, S. J. (1980). *Recording: Guidelines for social workers.* New York: MacMillan.

Katherine Dunlap wishes to thank Dr. Samuel D. Watson, Jr., University Writing Programs, UNC Charlotte, and Dr. Rachel Dedmon, School of Social Work, University of North Carolina at Chapel Hill, for reviewing earlier versions of the manuscript.

PART III

COPING
WITH
CHALLENGES

PART III: COPING WITH CHALLENGES

Now you've prepared yourself and you're ready to survive anything your field placement puts in front of you. But what are some of the challenges that lie ahead? They will be different for everyone, and you won't be able to fully anticipate them until you experience them firsthand.

You can prepare for concrete concerns, such as concerns for safety, by finding out what precautions and policies the field placement agency has in place. You can anticipate clinical challenges, such as vicarious traumatization or countertransference, by reading as much as you can about these issues.

Once you're in your placement, you can continue to face these challenges by discussing them with your field instructor. If problems persist, talk to the faculty liaison or other contacts at your school to resolve them. You will need to sort out which challenges are *problems,* and which are *necessary learning experiences.*

If you find that you are *not* challenged at all (or enough) during your field placement, talk to your field instructor, field seminar instructor, and/or field liaison. We've all heard the phrase, "If it seems too good to be true, it probably is." If your placement seems "too easy," then maybe it is. Assess whether you are learning anything new. If not, you may need to adjust your learning plan.

The problem-solving process is an important part of your field placement experience. Learning from it will help you to be the great social worker that you want to be.

10

Concerns in the Field Placement

by Joan Ferry DiGuilio, Ph.D., LISW

After completing extensive coursework, observing practice, and serving as a volunteer, you enter your field placement. This can be an opportunity to integrate theory into practice, try on various helping roles, become acculturated into the profession, and replace passive learning with active, professional work. While this sounds promising, you may also experience self doubt, anxiety, and unsureness. There are many things to learn and new situations to encounter in a short period of time: an unfamiliar agency, clients with pressing problems, and unknown co-workers.

Just what are the concerns of students in the field? In an attempt to answer this question, I conducted a study over a five-year period of time. During that time, I served as a faculty field work coordinator and taught the weekly field seminar class where students turned in journals. The daily entries from 214 students' journals were examined, subjected to content analysis, and categorized into areas of concern. Four major areas emerged: work environment concerns, supervisory concerns, client treatment concerns, and personal awareness issues.

Work Environment

A major concern expressed by students was the issue of safety on the job and in making home visits. Name calling, verbal threats, and being physically pushed by clients occurred more often than expected. One student was choked by a violent chronically mentally ill client. She managed to break loose by using self defense techniques learned in a university physical education class. Using "street smart" wisdom paid off for students who planned home visits for early mornings, locked car doors, traveled without a purse or briefcase, and took on an assertive "I know where I'm going" demeanor.

Liability issues were frequently mentioned. Students voiced concern over transporting clients in their cars, wondering what would happen in the event of an accident or injury. Wear and tear on the student's car and not being reimbursed for mileage were additional worries. Questions were also raised about liability for injuries the client or student might receive when attempting to restrain a client.

Agency politics were overwhelming to some students. Their idealism and fervor for the profession did not prepare them for rivalries and jealousies between workers, and between workers and administrators. A few students were shocked when field instructors limited opportunities to work with other staff members because of personal grudges. Conflict with agency staff was troublesome. Being considered "only a student" and receiving assignments that no one else wanted were specified. On several occasions, students were bothered that non-social work professionals at the field site did not understand social work or devalued it and glorified their own profession.

Supervision

Fear of approaching the field instructor for additional guidance and more varied assignments was problematic. Many students wanted strict, rigorous supervision that was characterized by regular, scheduled meetings, preliminary agendas, and detailed recordings. But they were hesitant to ask, since they did not wish to increase the work of the field instructor, whom they believed was already burdened with heavy work demands. Students were unsure about how to handle disagreement with the field instructor. The realization that the field instructor recommended their grade made some students ill at ease in being assertive or confronting.

In situations where students worked on projects under the tutelage of other staff, several students reported poor communication about the student's performance between the field instructor and the other staff. Consequently, the students believed that their evaluation was not representative of their accomplishments.

Client Treatment

While coursework addressed difficulties in dealing with manipulative, resistive, and multi-problem clients, few students felt prepared or confident of their work in these areas. Students reported feeling overwhelmed, becoming mistrustful, and questioning their ability to help others. They did not expect clients to reject their efforts to be helpful or to have an agenda that greatly differed from their own. Client self-determination was a principle that students incorporated into their learning. However, the injurious results of self-determination were not anticipated in situations when clients refused to take medications, or when they insisted on independent living arrangements when they were unable to perform tasks of daily living and lacked a support system.

Since many students worked in field agencies that were close to their homes, the issue of personally knowing clients was prominent. If the agency employed a small number of staff, transfer to another worker was not always feasible. Students needed to develop skills in sorting out client feelings and their own comfort-discomfort level when the client was their neighbor.

Termination proved to be a wrenching experience for some students. These students wanted to keep in touch with clients once their field placements ended. They viewed this as caring and being concerned and needed to address agency liability issues and promising clients more than they could deliver.

Personal Awareness

Students reported having dormant personal issues and feelings reawakened by clients' situations, such as death, alcoholism, or abuse. Younger students encountered overpowering helplessness when exposed to client life situations that were unfamiliar and tragic. Dealing with client racism and sexism challenged students. An African-American student commented on the anger she felt when an elderly nursing home client insisted that she perform housekeeping duties, but did not have these same expectations for White social workers. A female student found it difficult to tolerate a male client's deprecation and sexual innuendo. Finding the appropriate amount of self disclosure was a problem. Students who revealed too much commented on feeling a role reversal had taken place. Students who rarely self-disclosed mentioned feeling "wooden" and unconnected.

Coping With Concerns

What can you do if you are having concerns similar to those mentioned by the students in the study? First of all, remember that this is your learning experience. Take charge and shape it to fit your needs. You might want to consider the following suggestions.

- Find out if your field agency has a safety training program. If it does, sign up and participate.

- Consider enrolling in a self defense course at your university.

- Consult with your faculty field coordinator and agency field instructor about liability insurance and workers' compensation.

- Keep the lines of communication open between you and your field instructor. Remember, your goal is to maximize learning.

- Work out a supervisory plan that is agreeable to both you and your field instructor.

- Initiate three-way meetings for you, your field instructor, and any agency staff with whom you are working.

- Remember that client self-determination includes the right to reject your help.

- Use your inner feelings as a gauge. They are trying to tell you something about yourself.

- Get in touch with old, troublesome feelings and try to master them.

- Foster a life away from your work.

As a final note, nurture your enthusiasm and see each experience as growth producing. This can be one of the best times in your career.

Recommended Reading

Collins, D., Thomlison, B., & Grinnell, R. (1992). *The social work practicum: A student guide.* Itasca, IL: F.E. Peacock Publishers.

Royse, D., Dhooper, S. S., & Rompf, E. L. (1996). *Field instruction: A guide for social work students.* White Plains, NY: Longman.

Schneck, D., Grossman, B., & Glassman, U. (1990). *Field education in social work: Contemporary issues and trends.* Dubuque, IA: Kendall/Hunt.

Urbanowski, M. & Dwyer, M. (1988). *Learning through field instruction: A guide for teachers and students.* Milwaukee, WI: Family Service America.

11

Be Careful, It's a Jungle Out There: A Look at Risks in Field Placement

by Gregory R. Versen, MSSW, ACSW

"Be careful—it's a Jungle out there!" This phrase was part of each opening scene from the television series *Hill Street Blues.* The sergeant issued this warning to his charges at the Los Angeles police department as they left the briefing room to carry out the day's activities. This same warning can apply to students in field placement.

The voice on the phone was a familiar one. She was a graduate of our program, had gone on for a master's degree, and was now serving as an agency supervisor. It's what she said after the greeting that made my heart jump into my throat. "Kelly has been bitten by a dog!" The student was on a home visit and no one would answer the front door. As she moved to the back door, a German Shepherd met her coming around the corner. In this case, Kelly and the supervisor were making the home visit together, but that was not enough to keep it from happening. The bite was not serious, but definitely left an impression on her—and me.

During a recent semester, as I read the weekly journal of a student who was placed at a state psychiatric hospital, my pulse rate began to race as she described a situation where she found herself isolated in the facility's library with a male patient. She had been walking through the library to go to another part of the hospital when he grabbed her, forced her against a wall, and began touching her. She broke loose and found her supervisor. She was shaken but unharmed.

Such was not the case for MSW student Rebecca Ann Binkowski at Western Michigan University in 1993. She was working as resident manager at an apartment complex for clients with mental health problems. She was murdered by one of the residents.

The field practicum represents the capstone experience for social work students. It is here that one can demonstrate what has been learned after years of study and preparation, with real people who have real problems. The question is, "Have students been adequately prepared for everything they will encounter in the field?"

The above experiences involving students, in combination with a faculty meeting in which the issue of liability was discussed, made it clear that students were not entering the field practicum adequately informed of the risks they might encounter.

Being forewarned is being forearmed. An ounce of prevention is worth a pound of cure. These are the truisms that apply to the field practicum. Students entering the practicum will encounter situations that put them at risk, and it is important to be aware of them, so as to avoid them or to reduce as much as possible any negative experiences that might happen.

To address this concern, the Department of Social Work at James Madison University developed an *Assumption of Risk Statement* that students review and sign with the Director of Field Placement. They keep a copy, and a copy is kept in their permanent files. This statement identifies eight areas the faculty believe students need to be aware of as they begin their field experience.

Professional Liability Insurance

Many schools provide professional liability insurance to students who are enrolled in the school and are completing their educational requirements in a field practicum agency. If students are uncertain about this, they should consult with the director of field placement or department head. Even if students are covered by the school, it is recommended that they carry professional liability insurance over and above that provided through existing university policy.

Professional liability insurance can be purchased through student membership in the National Association of Social Workers (NASW) for a modest fee. JMU's program has never had a liability issue in its 30-year history. However, with the increasingly litigious nature of our society, JMU wants students to be covered, just in case.

As part of professional practice, it is important that students know the limits of their knowledge and skills and avoid helping situations that are not within their areas of competence. Whenever students have questions about the handling of a particular case or whether a given intervention is appropriate, it is their responsibility to consult with their supervisors.

Automobile Liability Insurance

For those students who use their personal vehicles in the field practicum, it is recommended that they check with their insurance company for a clear understanding of what coverage they have. Ask specifically what coverage you have if something happens while transporting a client. JMU recommends that students not use their personal vehicles to transport clients. If clients need to be transported, use agency vehicles.

TB Skin Test (PPD-S)

In recent years, there has been a surge in cases of tuberculosis. A recent *Newsweek* article on immigration stated, "Surveys of California's Asian and Central American immigrants have found that as many as 70% arrive carrying the germ that causes tuberculosis."

A colleague at another school shared an incident in which a student was exposed to TB. The student then exposed other students, resulting in widespread testing at the school.

Because of the highly contagious nature of TB, it is recommended that students be tested for it prior to entering the field. This is particularly important if the clients to be served are at risk for this disease. It is a simple and painless test that can be administered at the university health center, local health department, or family physician's office at nominal cost.

Client Office Visits

Meeting with clients in an office is an experience most field students will encounter with no problems. However, it can happen that a client may become agitated, hostile, or threatening during the interview. It is important that students discuss such matters with the agency supervisor early in the practicum, to be informed of agency policy and recommended courses of action should such an event ever happen. Never take risks with a client who becomes threatening. Leave the room and seek assistance.

Institutional Settings

Mental health and correctional settings serve client populations whose behavior may be unpredictable. It is important to learn strategies for handling clients whose behavior becomes threatening, especially if they touch or grab you. It is acceptable to request that your supervisor or another staff person accompany you when meeting with such persons.

Home Visits

It is not uncommon for students in a variety of social service settings to conduct home visits. Such visits do expose one to risks. It is important that all home visits be made with the full knowledge of your agency supervisor—time of departure, time of return, other activities while on the trip, and so on. Do not conduct a home visit when you feel uncomfortable or threatened. This also applies when you detect client use of drugs or alcohol. Return to the agency and report your experiences to your supervisor.

Another hazard of home visits is the dog or other household pet that might be a threat. If you are unable to get the client to restrict the animals so they no longer pose a danger to you, reschedule the visit. Also, know who to call or what steps to take if you should experience a vehicle breakdown.

After Hours Meetings

Some social service settings have activities that occur beyond normal office hours. Be aware of the location or neighborhood where such meetings take place, note street lighting, open spaces, shrubs, and other growth that might impair your vision. It is suggested that the student always be accompanied by a supervisor or someone else when going to a car after dark.

Hepatitis B Vaccine

If the student anticipates a placement setting where there is the chance of being exposed to blood-borne pathogens, it is recommended that they get the Hepatitis B vaccination. This process involves a series of three injections given over a six-month period of time and costs from $90-150. Because of the time involved, it is important that students anticipating a practicum in such a setting begin the vaccination series early enough to insure protection when they enter the field. Students are advised to continue to take precautions to protect themselves against these diseases.

The field practicum is one of the most exciting aspects of social work education. It is a time for personal and professional growth, for taking risks, learning limits, and setting boundaries. The challenge is to know which risks to take and which to avoid.

12

Vicarious Traumatization in Field Placements

by Randee Huber, MSW

I did a field placement with a group Post Traumatic Stress Disorder (PTSD) program. From almost the first day, clients with PTSD were all I cared about. Nothing else mattered. After hearing the things I heard every day, everything else was petty, and shallow, and pointless. I spent every day immersed in life-and-death situations. What was my life compared to that?

I had no life other than my practicum. My husband knew something was wrong, but I discounted him because I thought I knew more about it than he did. My sister knew, and I discounted her for the same reason. I look back now, and I can see clearly what I couldn't see then. I was obsessed. I was ill. I was suffering from secondary trauma.

When the placement was over and I realized I couldn't function, I began seeing a therapist who had a great deal of experience working with trauma. The first time I saw her, she told me I might want to do some reading about vicarious traumatization. This article was the result. I hope it might be helpful to other students who find themselves in this situation.

> *...over a large range of cases our ordinary thinking about morality assigns no positive value to the well-being or happiness of the moral agent of the sort it clearly assigns to the well-being or happiness of everyone other than the agent (Slote, 1993, p. 441, quoted in Shay, 1995, p.255).*

Not every field placement runs a great risk of putting students in harm's way. But it could be postulated that there might be at least some risk in many placements. One such risk is that of secondary trauma in students working with trauma survivors. Secondary trauma (also called vicarious traumatization; some authors make a distinction between the two terms, but they are usually used interchangeably) is considered to be virtually inevitable among those who work with victims of trauma, and may be particularly severe in students and inexperienced practitioners. Kelly Chrestman's study found that "less experienced therapists suffered the greatest distress" (1995, p. 34).

Stories about negligence, exploitation, and abuse are gut wrenching and heart breaking not only because of the pain to the victim. They are unbearable because they're so common. The monolithic social forces that allow, if not demand, that we hurt each other are too huge and overwhelming to contemplate.

Rosenbloom, Pratt, and Pearlman (1995) believe "It is important to emphasize that such responses on the part of the helper are not viewed as pathological; just as PTSD is viewed as a normal reaction to an abnormal event, vicarious traumatization is a normal reaction to the stressful and sometimes traumatizing work with victims" (p. 67).

The literature on secondary trauma is replete with symptoms that are common among therapists working with trauma survivors. They include (among others) a decreased sense of trust, shifts in beliefs and personality, feelings of being constantly threatened by potential harm, doubts about professional efficacy, a decreased sense of connection with others and social withdrawal, and judgment "impaired by disrupted beliefs that result in an inability to foresee consequences accurately" (Pearlman & Saakvitne, 1995, pp. 162-163).

Helpers may begin to see other people and the world as dangerous and threatening, malevolent and evil, untrustworthy and unreliable, exploitative and controlling, and/or disconnected and alienating. Like their clients, helpers may find their basic assumptions shattered (Rosenbloom, et al., 1995, p. 69).

This article has two purposes with regard to vicarious, or secondary, trauma. First is to educate readers about it, and second is the responsibility of schools of social work and field agencies to warn and educate their students about potential risks of personal harm—risks to well-being and happiness—in field placements, and what they can do to ameliorate those risks.

Duty to Warn

Duty to warn has been discussed in the literature on secondary trauma. Figley (1995) said, "We must do all we can to insure that trauma workers are prepared...we have a 'duty to inform' them about the hazards of this work" (p. 22). Munroe (1995) added, "...not only should we be concerned about warning candidates of the potential harm of being exposed to trauma, but...we should also train them how to cope with this exposure" (p. 215) and, "Conspicuously absent from the ethical codes is the welfare of the therapist" (p. 225).

If schools of social work and field agencies believe that it is important for students to learn and understand the concepts of duty to warn and informed consent, do they also have a moral imperative to extend those ideas to their students? The NASW *Code of Ethics*, with regard to education, states that educators and field instructors "should provide instruction only within their areas of knowledge and competence," and based on current information, that they should evaluate students fairly, that they should inform clients when services are being provided by students, and that they should not engage in dual or multiple relationships with students (1996, p. 19). The *Code of Ethics* discusses at length the social worker's responsibilities with regard to obtaining informed consent from clients (1996, pp. 7-8). But nowhere does it address responsibilities to warn students of potential harm, or to obtain informed consent from them.

Coping with Secondary Trauma

Secondary trauma is exacerbated if it is unrecognized. Sometimes therapists can be so immersed in their own trauma and its effects that they don't want to see it in a colleague. When a therapist has been traumatized by his or her work with a trauma survivor client, it is inevitably a disturbing event for his or her professional peers. The simple occurrence of this event is a reminder to all other therapists that they too are vulnerable. One way to defend against this experience of vulnerability is to view the event as something peculiar to the particular therapist involved, rather than to the work itself.

This manner of defending against the experience of heightened vulnerability is usually manifested by a distancing reaction—for example, the traumatized therapist is viewed as not functioning well because of something being wrong *with* him or her rather than something having happened *to* him or her (Catherall, 1995, p. 87).

In his chapter titled "Coping with Secondary Traumatic Stress: The Importance of the Therapist's Professional Peer Group," Don R. Catherall explains how effective trauma peer groups work, and why they sometimes do not. When the defensive view that the affected individual is only affected because he or she is different in the first place gains prominence within the group, the traumatized individual is left feeling alienated, vulnerable, and personally damaged. This social cutoff then constitutes an additional trauma, a *relational trauma,* which exacerbates the original stress response. If the affected member can be pushed out of the group— either physically or psychologically—then the other members of the group are more able to maintain the illusion that they are free from the threat of traumatization (Catherall, 1995, p. 87-88).

When this happens, the worker is not only traumatized by working with trauma survivors; she is also traumatized by her interactions with the team. For an intern, who is already in a peripheral role with the team, it can be devastating.

The Team and Supervision

Munroe and colleagues, in "Preventing Compassion Fatigue: A Team Treatment Model," describe a "treatment team" model that, if it's done right, may work. However, it is detrimental if it's done wrong.

Team cohesiveness may lead to an unspoken desire for unanimity . . . Dangers include the development of stereotyped views of other groups, self-censorship of deviations from group consensus, and the exclusion of information or persons not in accord with the group consensus . . . Persons with minority opinions or special knowledge may be discounted because of a subtle threat to group conformity. Although a team may outwardly value and ask for alternative opinions, there may exist a subtle and covert pres-

sure to maintain unanimity . . . . [W]e took very seriously a reference to the team as a cult. It is possible for an entire team to be engaged in a trauma pattern (Munroe, et al, 1995 p.227).

The field supervisor's inevitable position as part of the team contributes to problems for the student. In her discussion of field supervisors of student interns, Nora Bonosky writes, "Social workers need to come to grips with their own vulnerability.... They must work toward the same kind of self-awareness, introspection, and openness to growth that is asked of students. Professionals need to remain continuously cognizant of the whole range of conflicts, paradoxes, distortions, prejudices, and hidden agendas in their value and belief systems.... [S]upervisors, first of all, must be relentless about the monitoring of their own unconscious processes" (1995, p. 91).

If the supervisor is driven to "maintain [team] unanimity" and is unwilling to recognize his own vulnerability to trauma, he is not being relentless about monitoring his own unconscious processes, no matter what he may believe to the contrary. When the supervisor is not "cognizant of the whole range of conflicts, paradoxes, distortions, prejudices, and hidden agendas" in his own belief system and that of the team, the supervisee is at risk.

In this situation, the student may very likely begin to distrust his or her supervisor. Cathy Jacobs, quoting Pinderhughs (1989, p.11), writes, "A supervisor may use the 'helping' role to reinforce...[his or her] own sense of competence by keeping subordinates in a one-down position" (1991, p. 130). Jacobs continues, "Students who are devalued, humiliated, coerced, frightened, ignored, or criticized in a nonconstructive way by supervisors are unlikely to protest because of their power disadvantage.... Thus, supervisors can refute or pathologize student reactions, including healthy assertive behaviors, without threatening their own reputations or institutional base of support. As "experts," their power advantage includes enhanced credibility" (1991, p. 130).

If a student's symptoms are creating a problem for her, and these problems are unrecognized, ignored, or discounted by her supervisor (and the rest of the team, if this is the model being used), her power disadvantage leaves her with few options, and she will in all likelihood not feel safe telling the supervisor the things she needs to tell him.

Preparing Students

Students usually enter a placement with expectations of learning a great deal and receiving good supervision. If they enter the placement with no intimate knowledge of trauma work, and with no knowledge of secondary trauma, they will not know that they are vulnerable to vicarious traumatization, as all therapists who work with trauma survivors are. They will not know how to recognize it or what to do about it. They need to be told and educated about secondary trauma either by the university or by the PTSD program staff, or both.

Catherall says, "This possibility [of secondary trauma] is best discussed within the group *before it occurs....* [I]t is advisable that the group spend some time discussing the likelihood of secondary traumatization (1995, p.88)." Munroe suggests that therapists working with victims of trauma have a "duty to warn...when hiring or assigning a new therapist to work with trauma clients" (1995, p. 213-214), of the risk of secondary trauma. Even if students read on their own about therapeutic group processes or PTSD, they will probably not find the terms "secondary trauma" or "vicarious traumatization" in the literature they choose to read.

The Ethics of Preparation

A search of *Social Work Abstracts* found 106 entries on "ethics and education." Only three of them were about ethical education. If social workers have an ethical responsibility to warn their clients of potential harm, to inform them of risks, and to "do no harm," then schools of social work, and their field agencies, have an ethical responsibility to extend these principles to their students.

Gelman, Pollack, and Auerbach (1996) write, "If harm befalls a social work student while at a field placement, can the school be held liable? If the school voluntarily fosters the expectation that it is responsible for the safety of its students while they are at their field placements, liability might follow" (p. 352). If a school requires field work, procures field placements, and sends its students to work there, there is an implicit expectation that the placement is safe. Liability aside, is it morally and ethically valid to send students into situations where they will *not* be safe? The answer is obviously "No."

Since field work is required, placements are solicited by the school, and the assignment made with (often) little input from the student, the school is voluntarily fostering the expectation that it is responsible for the student's safety. Gelman and Wardell (1988) recommend that students' informed consent be sought with regard to field placements. "Students should not become victims in the process or be asked to assume unreasonable risks" (p. 77).

However, if the field agency is not forthcoming about risks to the student, it too is responsible, should harm result. "The field office and field agencies also need to establish policies to protect students from foreseeably dangerous situations," according to Zakutansky & Sirles (1993, p. 343). They add, "By offering placements in such facilities [where there is risk of harm], field instructors must accept the responsibility for teaching awareness and management of the risks inherent to dangerous situations" (p. 342). If, in the case of secondary trauma, the field instructor is so enmeshed in his own secondary trauma that he is unable or unwilling to see it as a hazard, then the placement is not safe for interns.

Given the moral, ethical, and legal demands incumbent upon schools of social work, if students who have done placements that have caused them harm have informed their school of social work of the potential risks of these placements, and the school has not informed students who are subsequently assigned to these placements of the risks, or, more astutely, removed these agencies as placements, an assumption of reckless disregard does not seem misplaced.

Protecting Yourself

If field agencies and schools do not take responsibility for protecting students, then students need to protect themselves. I suggest that students ask about potential risks associated with field placements, and get them in writing, both from the school and the agency. My hope is that schools will warn students of the risk of secondary trauma, just as they would warn them of other risks. I suggest students do as much reading and research about their placements as possible, and I hope that, when appropriate, they will be directed to readings that will educate them about secondary trauma.

I also suggest that students who will be working with trauma survivors (and this includes abused children, battered women, combat veterans, adult survivors of sexual abuse, rape victims, and others), if at all possible, have a therapist to talk to while doing their placements, and that they read as much as possible about secondary trauma and make themselves aware of the symptoms. (Saakvitne and Pearlman's book *Transforming the Pain* is very helpful, as is Kelly Chrestman's (1994) dissertation on secondary trauma, which includes several trauma symptom checklists). And students who will be working with trauma survivors should discuss secondary trauma with the field supervisor prior to accepting the placement to be sure he or she is cognizant of its existence, symptoms, prevention, and treatment.

References

Bonosky, N. (1995). Boundary violations in social work supervision: Clinical, educational, and legal implications. *Clinical Supervisor, 13 (2)*, 79-95.

Catherall, D. R. (1995). Coping with traumatic stress: The importance of the therapist's professional peer group. In B. H. Stamm (Ed.). *Secondary traumatic stress: Self-care issues for clinicians, researchers, and educators.* Lutherville, MD: Sidran Press.

Chrestman, K. R., (1994). *Secondary traumatization in therapists working with survivors of trauma.* Doctoral dissertation, Nova University.

Chrestman, K. R., (1995). Secondary exposure to trauma and self reported distress among therapists. In B. H. Stamm (Ed.). *Secondary traumatic stress: Self-care issues for clinicians, researchers, and educators.* Lutherville, MD: Sidran Press.

Figley, C.R., (1995). Compassion fatigue: Toward a new understanding of the costs of caring. In B. H. Stamm (Ed.), *Secondary traumatic stress: Self-care issues for clinicians, researchers, and educators.* Lutherville, MD: Sidran Press.

Gelman, S. R., Pollack, D., & Auerbach, C. (1996). Liability issues in social work education. *Journal of Social Work Education, 32 (3)*, 351-361.

Gelman, S.R. & Wardell, P.J. (1988). Who's responsible? The field liability dilemma. *Journal of Social Work Education, 24 (1)*, 70-78.

Jacobs, C. (1991). Violations of the supervisory relationship: An ethical and educational blind spot. *Social Work, 36 (2)*, 130-135.

Munroe, J. F. (1995). Ethical issues associated with secondary stress in therapists. In B. H. Stamm (Ed.). *Secondary traumatic stress: Self-care issues for clinicians, researchers, and educators.* Lutherville, MD: Sidran Press.

Munroe, J. F., Shay, J., Fisher, L., Makary, C., Rapperport, K., & Zimering, R. (1995). Preventing compassion fatigue: A team treatment model. In C. R. Figley (Ed.). *Compassion fatigue: Coping with secondary traumatic stress disorder in those who treat the traumatized.* New York: Brunner/Mazel.

National Association of Social Workers (1996). *Code of Ethics.* Washington, D.C.: Author.

Pearlman, L. A., & Saakvitne, K.W. (1995). Treating therapists with vicarious traumatization and secondary traumatic stress disorder. In C. R. Figley (Ed.). *Compassion fatigue: coping with secondary traumatic stress disorder in those who treat the traumatized.* New York: Brunner/Mazel.

Rosenbloom, D., Pratt, A. C., & Pearlman, L. A. (1995). Helpers' responses to trauma work: Understanding and intervening in an organization. In B. H. Stamm (Ed.), *Secondary traumatic stress: Self-care issues for clinicians, researchers, and educators.* Lutherville, MD: Sidran Press.

Shay, J. (1995). No escape from philosophy in trauma treatment and research. In B. H. Stamm (Ed.). *Secondary traumatic stress: self-care issues for clinicians, researchers, and educators.* Lutherville, MD: Sidran Press.

Zakutansky, T. J. & Sirles, E. A. (1993). Ethical and legal issues in field education: Shared responsibility and risk. *Journal of Social Work Education, 29 (3),* 338-347.

13

When the Change Agent Experiences Unplanned Change

by Denice Goodrich Liley, Ph.D., ACSW

Social workers are referred to as "change agents," because we are specifically employed for the purposes of helping to bring about planned changes in our clients' lives, changes that may affect individuals, families, groups, or communities. Social work education centers on "others' change," yet rarely do we explore how change affects the change agent.

You will most likely face the first of many professional challenges with change when selecting, beginning, or experiencing field placement. You have worked long and hard to reach your practicum experience, and field placement may be the first opportunity for you to provide input in shaping your professional education. Fieldwork will be full of firsts: agency responsibilities, real clients, real challenges, as well as your own perceptions and expectations about what is social work practice.

Field instruction is viewed as the capstone of social work education, bridging together the experiential with the theoretical underpinnings of practice. This is the arena in which you will experience an integration of theoretical knowledge with actual case material. You will acquire experience in assessment skills, in selecting models of treatment, and in testing intervention strategies. The concepts, principles, and theories discussed in the classroom will come to life for you. Both at the bachelor's and at the master's levels, students of social work usually describe their practicum as the single most useful, significant, and powerful learning experience of their formal education. Therefore, the selection of a field practicum is a major consideration for every student.

This combination of firsts, which occurs at the culmination of your formal course work, along with the emphasis that social work education places on the experience, causes students to view any change in field practicum as catastrophic. Yet, as with any other real world experience, change is what you will most likely encounter as you step into the field.

Change Happens

We commonly define change as "to put or take something in place of something else; to exchange, to make different, a substitution, alteration, or a variation." Social workers are well versed at the "how-to" level when it comes to helping others institute changes. Additionally, social work students are cautioned about professional stress and burnout. These have little relevance, though, to the social work student. All too often, disillusionment with the social work profession can be tied to the outgrowths of students' experiences with change that they have had no opportunity to discuss with others, and in reality, we give little attention to what to do when the change involves the social worker's life.

The social work education process prepares you to facilitate for others in implementing planned changes in their lives, but what happens when the change agents are faced with their own changes?

Educators discuss the types of differences social workers may experience in fieldwork, such as differences in values, culture, or beliefs; however, little attention is given to encountering experiential changes. We seem to acquire the belief that change is a given in the world with which we will be associated, and that in some way we will have absorbed the "how-to" skills to manage it. On the other hand, perhaps we simply overlook emphasizing that social workers will also face unplanned change.

Common Reactions to Change

Social workers react no differently to change than do our clients. For instance, you report to your fieldwork assignment to find the supervisor you were to be assigned to work with has been promoted and you will be working with another field supervisor. You may experience feelings of anger, resentment, and questions of "why me?" The difficulty exists in separating those feelings, reactions, and expectations from the reality of what exactly is the change. The high value placed on, along with the importance of, field practicum causes students to become intolerant of anything different. We then perceive the smallest of changes as earth shattering, equating the practicum as less than idealistic. We fear the unknown, and it becomes urgent that our coursework and field placement follow a schedule—a "planned" schedule. Typically, social work students have interviewed and carefully selected their field assignment. Then when faced with change, we decide all was for naught. We think, "I should have known better," or "Someone should have warned me."

Last minute changes can create it-has-to-be-all-or-nothing feelings of despair, such as, "Now all the good placements are gone." Or "I have to stay with this placement, because the only ones left must be bad—otherwise someone else would have already selected them."

When you experience change during field practicum, it hits at the core of change issues: Things are not what you expected. Field practicum in and of itself is a stressful experience. Change may cause you to feel as though you have been stripped of your own authentic choices.

Embrace the Change

Embrace the challenge to discover within yourself strategies to cope with the situation. Try this common approach: Think of the four R's: **React, Realistic, Recreate, Re-energize.** Begin by focusing your *reaction* to the change. Find someone who will allow you to vent all your feelings, thoughts, and concerns associated with the change. This will help you to move on. Ask yourself this question: "What does this change mean to me and my learning experience?" Practicum students are often unable to see the practicum director or a field liaison until they believe the worst possible case scenario is at hand. More often than not, the university will perceive the change as minor or as a good learning experience; however, students may not be informed about the change until field placement begins. The sense of not having a voice in the matter fuels the fire in reaction to the change, a reaction that may not in fact be to the change itself, but to not being considered and feeling as though our voice has been negated.

The second concept is to be *realistic*: What is the change? You may find that the person you wanted as a field instructor is no longer available, but remember to try to determine whether the personnel change makes a real difference in your field experience, and try to determine what those differences are. The changes may have no direct impact on you. Ask yourself whether you are more concerned with how others might perceive the change than the change itself. To move toward being realistic about the change, write out questions that you may want to ask of the university field director, field liaison, or field practicum instructor. What did you expect in your field practicum experience, and how is it different? In what specific ways will the change affect your learning experience?

Aim for *recreating*: Are there any benefits to the change? You may learn new approaches to try, you may have increased opportunity for experiences that are more varied or varied staff, or you may be given enlarged or expanded responsibilities as a result of the change. You may have the opportunity to become a specialist in a narrower field.

Change occurs, but what you do with the change is what really makes the difference. The change in practicum may in fact mean that you will have to move to a different agency to get the field practicum experience you desired. It is crucial to discuss this with your field director, field liaison, and the agency.

Finally, *re-energize*. Try to find ways to invest in the change. What benefits do you see in the change for yourself, your clients, or the systems you are working with? It is erroneous to not accept change. To feel you are just biding your time until graduation is wasted energy. Field practicum is an essential educational opportunity, one that requires investment of all parties—students, university, and field agency personnel—to be a successful venture. It is the crucial experience of tying everything together and gaining confidence in your professional skills and abilities.

Conclusion

Change is a reality. You will face changes throughout your professional career. Emotional reactions to change will occur. The suddenness and shock of the unexpected is natural. However, it is vital to move beyond reacting, to become realistic and explore ways to recreate learning opportunities through the change, and to re-energize yourself, so you can benefit from what you've invested in the field experience.

Field practicum is the ideal place for you to explore and refine your skills and strategies for change. All too often, we—students, university, and agency faculty—fail to explore those reactions. By emphasizing staying on track, we overlook exploring reactions, being realistic, recreating opportunities, and staying invested in the learning process.

You need a strong voice for yourself, as well as for your clients. It is important to develop interpersonal skills for dealing with change for yourself, your clients, your agency, and your community. Having those skills will empower you to provide a sense of control in the face of the unknown. Moreover, all changes cannot be planned changes—not even for the change agent!

14

My Practicum: Why Do I Hate It So?

and 5 steps toward making it more lovable

by Sondra J. Fogel, Ph.D., MSSW, ACSW

For many, the most exciting part of the social work curriculum is the actual practice of social work skills in the field practicum. Students are usually excited, anxious, and expecting this learning sequence to be the best time of their educational experience. However, this is not always the case. Field experiences create stress, pressures, doubts, anger, frustration, and tears. Students can feel lost and unprotected in this professional training segment that drastically differs from their previous educational experiences.

What Can Go Wrong?

To comprehend what can go wrong, it is important to understand how practicum sites are arranged. Field placements involve a matching process between learner needs as determined by the school and student specialization, and an agency setting that identifies opportunities and training personnel, i.e., an experienced social worker, to the university. Like all matches, there are many variables that affect a successful placement. For instance, the student and the field instructor have to be able to establish an effective supervisory style that promotes learning. Also, the agency has to be in a fairly secure position to provide consistent and appropriate tasks for the student. Finally, the student has to balance the roles of worker and apprentice in the university and agency setting.

For instance, Sarah, an African-American student, was delighted to work with at-risk middle school students in a dropout prevention program that utilized individual and group interventions. Furthermore, she was under the supervision of an experienced African-American MSW, a role model she wanted. Why was she not assigned cases, like her classmates in other placements? Didn't her field instructor like her? Her insecurities in her practice skills grew as her work was criticized and challenged by her instructor.

Mike, a non-traditional student, was placed in a grass-roots organization that used mostly older adult women volunteers to run a variety of programs for disenfranchised groups. When he interviewed for the site, he was told that he would work in a specific program. However, this was changed early in the placement when his field instructor asked him to work part-time in another program, in a different location. His daily supervisor in this setting was a para-professional volunteer from whom he felt he could not learn community organization skills. Organizational problems, particularly this volunteer, according to the student, impeded his ability to complete seminar assignments.

Joanne thought she would do fine in her placement in a child protective agency. Two other students were also placed in the same section and with the same field instructor. As the semester progressed, each student had a different relationship with the field instructor, despite everyone having the same number of cases. "No pain, no gain" became the theme of the field experience, with each student emerging from supervision with tears and self-doubts. Joanne wrote in her journal of her difficulties with the field instructor. Her seminar faculty provided responses to her concerns in her journal, but did not seem to do anything to help her. Joanne did marginal work in the placement, afraid of her field instructor and isolated from her seminar faculty.

These situations are true, and more common than we would like to admit. As the scenarios show, field problems include not being assigned cases, insecurity in practice skills, being criticized and changing supervisors, and interpersonal difficulties with field instructors. However, this is not an exhaustive list. Other issues may also cause problems, such as the student not knowing how to protect his or her boundaries in the setting, physical assaults by clients, passive-aggressive behavior by other staff members, sexual harassment, unleashing of personal issues brought up by increased self-awareness, and uncertainty of practice skills. No wonder then, some students ask, "Why do I hate this so?"

Consequences of Field Problems

When these or other difficulties in the practicum site occur, most students pass through a predictable stage. They will minimize the significance of the situation with coping thoughts like "It was just a bad day" or "It will only happen this once." Then, as uncomfortable feelings repeatedly occur, the issue is shared with family, significant others, or friends. By the time the field liaison or the seminar faculty learns about the problem, formal intervention is required. This might mean a call from the field liaison to the field instructor, or a written report on the student's performance by the field instructor to the field director. By this time, the student's anxiety level is high, as well as feelings of powerlessness and loss of control. Furthermore, it is not unlikely that the student with the field problem will be isolated, either intentionally or not, from other classmates.

This creates a very difficult experience for a student who is trying to gain the skills and identify with the values of social work. It is not unusual for students to wonder about their suitability for the profession based on difficulties in the practicum. The encouraging piece of news is that field difficulties and the associated feelings and patterns of student behaviors is not uncommon; rather it is normal and predictable to most field program staff.

Nonetheless, it must be acknowledged that problems can be indications of student unsuitability to the placement site and/or the profession. What does this mean? First one has to recognize that this is scary. Then, alternative options need to be generated for the student. This could mean moving the student to another type of practicum setting specializing in a different method of social work practice, or the student expectations and learning contract might be modified to reflect student ability, or a new field instructor may be recruited.

If a student learns during practicum that being a social worker is not what he or she really wants or can do, this is not a sign of failure. It is an indication of self-awareness. This should be celebrated. Knowing oneself is a strength that is highly valued in social work practice. As most experienced workers know, it is better to like or love what you are doing than to be miserable at the thought of going to work every day. The curriculum in accredited social work programs not only provides a general knowledge foundation applicable to most other educational vocations, but the communication and critical thinking skills mastered are transferable to most other professions.

Five Things You Can Do for an Effective Placement

By now, it is evident that placement is a minefield of potential problems in which most students experience some discomfort with various issues at different times. It is important to remember that even with problems, most students successfully complete placement and go on to be outstanding social work professionals. While no one can predict a placement outcome, below are five suggestions that might help minimize practicum troubles.

1. Know what you want to learn and tell this to the appropriate school personnel.

Remember, field placement, unlike your other classes, is a matching process of your interests, available sites and instructors, and school-agency connections. Unlike other relationships you are involved in, your choice in the selection event is limited. Therefore, it is imperative that you know what skills, knowledge, and values you want to work on in your placement.

What does this mean? First, you must know the type of population you want to work with and in what type of setting. You also have to know what your strengths are, as evidenced in your course work, particularly your methods classes. What are your weaknesses, and do you want to work on them? Tell this information to the appropriate field person in your school and during your placement interview, if you have one.

2. Know who you are. Do a thorough self-assessment.

Reflect on your previous group experiences and employment situations, and recognize the type of worker you are. What kind of person do you want to work with? In other words, how do you learn best—from someone who will tell you exactly what to do or from someone who will let you try things on your own? How do you handle criticism? Do you hear praise? How do you measure success? Do you work comfortably with all genders, ages, and races? What are your expectations? Look and know your history. And as mentioned above, tell this to the appropriate persons.

3. Understand and use the school field resources.

As social work students, you are encouraged to do a system analysis and understand how systems affect the individual. Remember that you are part of a system, the field placement system, which uses a variety of actors to accomplish the educational mission of the school. Get to know the roles of your field instructor, field director, seminar instructor/faculty and field liaison, and use them. These individuals invest in your success, but you must use them appropriately and according to school policies.

4. Don't blame—explain.

This is a very important point. Every field program has a policy that outlines what to do to inform and document field difficulties. Acknowledge that something may not be right early in the placement process and seek assistance by using the correct field person—your field instructor, seminar faculty, or field liaison. Do not be afraid to advocate for yourself in your field placement. This is not a sign of weakness in the learning process. It is an indication of professional development and maturity.

Furthermore, recognize that you and your field instructor may not get along on a personal level, but that doesn't mean you cannot learn and work together. There will be many times in your professional career when you will not like the person for whom you work, but you will like what you do. This is part of the reality of professional life. Be aware of this and distinguish between feelings on a personal level and practice on the professional side.

5. Be realistic.

Entering a field placement site requires that you and your field instructor discuss expectations concerning agency practices and politics, and your learning needs and goals. Remember that the purpose of the placement is for you to gain knowledge and experience with the social service system, and to develop your understanding of the social work role. To do this, it means you have to be prepared to be a professional. Do not plan to work many part-time hours outside of the agency while in the field practicum. Also, realize you probably will not socialize with the same frequency as you did in your earlier educational career. Expect to feel different from your friends and in limbo in the university system. Remember to work toward your educational goals and those that you set for yourself. Refer to Point One.

Ending with Success

Completing required field placement segments marks the transformation from student to social work professional. The experience guarantees to bring out your strengths and develop skills that you will consistently use in your daily practice. While it is common to think that when things go wrong in the setting, you are alone and powerless, remember, this is not true. Field departments are prepared to help you in your professional development. Your success is vitally important, not only to you but to your school and the profession.

Recommended Reading on Field Placement

Baird, B. (1996). *The internship, practicum, and field placement handbook: A guide for the helping professions.* Upper Saddle River, NJ: Prentice Hall.

Royse, D., Dhooper, S. S., & Rompf, E. L. (1996). *Field instruction: A guide for social work students.* New York: Longman Publishers.

PART IV

SUPERVISION AND EVALUATION

PART IV: SUPERVISION AND EVALUATION

You may have been supervised in the past—in a previous job, in an assistantship on campus, or somewhere else. Maybe you have supervised others, as well.

In a non-social work setting, the supervisor's job often revolves around making sure you get to work on time, don't goof off, and get the work done. In social work, all those things are extremely important. Supervision goes beyond the administrative end of things, though.

In field placement, your supervisor is more than a person you "report to" or refer to as your "boss." Supervision takes on a special role in your learning.

Notice that your supervisor is officially referred to as your *field instructor.* This person serves first and foremost as an educator in his or her relationship with you. The field instructor may also be a role model, a mentor, and a person who holds you accountable (and also may have some legal responsibility) for your actions.

You will find out the depth and importance of this relationship soon enough, from your own experience. You probably won't fully understand it until then. It is a crucial part of your practicum experience. Cherish it and nourish it to get the most out of your placement.

15

Preparing for Supervision

by Charles E. Floyd, Ph.D., LCSW

Cindy just started her first-year practicum, and tomorrow is her first weekly session with her agency field instructor. What should she talk about? What will the supervisor expect of her? What is this supervision all about, anyway?

Charles has been meeting with his supervisor on a regular basis, presenting cases, discussing agency policy issues, and evaluating progress toward his goals. He and his supervisor are reviewing a videotape of a session with a client. The supervisor, instead of talking about the client's issues, wants to know what was going through Charles' mind, how he felt about the client, and what he thinks his body language during this session meant. This makes Charles feel uncomfortable. The supervisor comments that Charles is squirming in his seat.

Traci's field instructor, Tom, is well-liked by everyone in the agency. It is mid-semester, and the practicum is going well. Traci is learning a lot and likes Tom's supervision style. He seems to understand her so well. One day he invites her to go to a popular local pub at the end of the day. Is this okay? she wonders.

These three vignettes illustrate three things that come to mind in considering the supervisory relationship between a student and field instructor:

1. What is the structure of the relationship?
2. What are the process dynamics of the relationship?

3. How do you make sure the relationship follows ethical guidelines?

As a student, you should consider each of these aspects when entering into supervision with a field instructor.

What is Supervision?

Supervision is the term generally used to refer to the supervisory relationship between student and field instructor. This relationship is characterized as a predominantly educationally-focused teaching relationship. If you are ill-prepared to use the educational dimension of the relationship, its complexity can easily confuse you. Just as easily, the educational focus may puzzle field instructors who then fall back on an employee-supervisor focus.

If you are a student with little or no work experience, you can draw on your classroom educational experiences to conceptualize the field instructor-student relationship. If you have a significant work history, you can use such experiences to form an idea of the supervision relationship.

You and your classmates may bring different ideas and perspectives on supervision depending on your backgrounds. Field instructors vary in their styles of supervision. One may be easy-going, while another is confrontational. These differences in perspective on the relationship, when brought together in the agency environment, form a unique context and expression of supervision. From this rich environment, the supervisory/teaching relationship unfolds.

Rich and complex variables influence the nature of the relationship between student and field instructor. Because of this complexity, a simple recipe for prescribing the best working relationship between student and field instructor becomes a complicated task. Significant interpersonal forces, individualized learning needs, and one's conceptual framework influence the supervision arrangement. In the midst of this complexity, you also need to be aware of the ethical considerations.

The following suggestions may help you think about your conceptualization of supervision. Keep in mind that there are probably as many variations in supervision as there are in social work practice models.

Structural Aspects of Supervision

Remember Cindy? She didn't know what to expect in her meetings with her field instructor. She and her supervisor had not yet set up a structure to follow. Perhaps that would be the agenda for that first supervision session.

Structure involves organizing your expectations and responsibilities. Begin by reading your school's field practicum manual. Clearly understand how the social work program defines your responsibilities and field instructor responsibilities. Develop a sense of the philosophical orientation of the program. To some extent, this is reflected by the organizing structure imposed by the school. Once this is understood, take a proactive position in structuring supervision to meet your needs.

Schools often use tools such as educational contracts, recording requirements, and specific supervisory techniques to structure supervision.

Educational Contracts

Your school may expect students to actively participate with their field instructors in preparing an educational contract or learning plan. The quality of these contracts varies. Beyond spelling out learning objectives, your educational contract should define certain aspects of the supervisory relationship. Before preparing the contract, you should know something about your learning style, know what kind of supervision you like, and have some idea of your field instructor's supervisory style.

Identify specific learning assignments and how they relate to specific learning objectives. Learning assignments and supervisory-teaching methods should reflect both your and your field instructor's needs. If possible, include the time, day, place, and frequency of scheduled supervision.

Spell out mutual supervision expectations in the educational contract. This can prevent potential problems with the supervisory relationship. Find out what the field instructor expects you to bring into supervision. You should be prepared to bring in questions, problems, and a report of how you are using your time. Find out if there is a particular sequential focus to the supervision. Think of the educational contract as the structural foundation of the supervisory relationship. This approach can be helpful in learning the role and usefulness of contracting with clients. Contracting is key to setting supervision structure.

Recording Supervision

Keeping weekly supervisory notes can be extremely helpful in adding structure to supervision. Encourage your field instructor to keep notes as well. Notes should include the date of the supervision, the focus of the supervision, the field instructor's feedback, and notes on discussion of issues related to specific learning objectives, ethical/value issues, policy matters, special populations, and cultural diversity. Note if there are any changes in the focus or direction of learning assignments.

Some social work programs use journals and/or other written assignments, such as process recording, to supplement field instruction. Use written materials as a way of monitoring the focus and effectiveness of supervision and measuring your learning progress.

Supervision Tools and Techniques

Tools may include audio and video taping, process recording, journals, shadowing, role playing, case presentations, and observation. To some extent, the use of these tools and techniques depends on the resources available, the field instructor's familiarity and comfort, and what works best for both you and the field instructor. Talk with your field instructors to determine what might work best; experiment and self-evaluate.

Process Aspects of Supervision

In the example at the beginning of this article, Charles felt okay talking about client problems and agency rules, but got uncomfortable when his supervisor confronted him about his own reactions during the therapeutic and supervisory processes.

The interactional or process part of the supervisory relationship with your field instructor is an important part of your learning. This is a challenging area, because process issues can easily turn into therapy or other boundary intrusions.

Several qualities influence the relationship; some of these qualities include the presence and degree of mutuality, reciprocity, collaboration, trust, respect, and open communication. Though the supervisory relationship should not include "therapy," you can use the process dimension of supervision to gain self knowledge and increased awareness.

In the process dimension, you can learn more fully how to use self in a helping relationship. As important, you gain awareness as to how you use yourself in present moment-to-moment supervisory interaction between you and your field instructor. As you are presenting a case to your field instructor, you might notice that you, like Charles, become uncomfortable. Maybe your voice drops to a soft, nearly inaudible level, and you are avoiding eye contact with your supervisor. Experiment with giving some attention to your immediate experience. You may decide to risk shifting the focus to your experience of presenting the case and exploring how this might relate to your work with the client. Attending to your immediate experiences can expand your awareness of your communication style.

Ethical Concerns

The school and, to some extent, the professional organization (NASW) define the formal relationship between you and the field instructor. As a student, you are in a formalized hierarchical power relationship with a professional social worker designated as your field instructor. Your central role in the relationship is as student. Although you are not a "client" of the field instructor, you and the field instructor should avoid multiple relationships. Keep the relationship in the context of student-field instructor.

The social work profession considers "teaching" as practice, though it doesn't require one to be licensed. Most, if not all, schools are exempt from licensing requirements, and social work faculty generally aren't required to have a license. On the other hand, field instructors are generally employed as practitioners and as such, are bound by the licensing requirements for practitioners in the state in which they practice.

In the context of teaching as social work practice, be aware of the ethical boundaries of the supervisory relationship with your field instructor. Take some time to review the National Association of Social Workers' Code of Ethics (1996), Section II, Item 4. It cautions social workers that they should avoid "dual or multiple relationships with clients...."

Involvement beyond a teaching relationship is not necessarily unethical. However, as a student in a hierarchical power relationship, you are vulnerable to potential exploitation.

Take the case of Traci and her supervisor, Tom. Traci has to ask herself (or Tom)—what is Tom's motivation in asking her to go out to the pub? And what is Traci's motivation in accepting? If the purpose is to solidify the learning relationship or to discuss professional issues, it may be okay. If there are personal motivations involved, it's not such a good idea.

As a social work student, it is appropriate for you to bring up the issue of "dual relationships" and reach an understanding with your field instructor. Above all else, it is important to stay within clear professional boundaries to avoid potentially conflicting roles and interests. Wininger (1995) mentions this ethical issue in a proposed student code of ethics.

In time, supervisory relationships eventually change to collegial relationships. With this transition, the relationship extends to new boundaries. However, during the course of formal supervision, explicit boundaries must be observed.

If your school has not addressed these matters in its field practicum manual, advocate for their inclusion in the manual, and refer to NASW's supervision guidelines for guidance. At a minimum, consider applying the following NASW clinical supervision guidelines, which have been adapted for the practicum setting:

1. Work with your field instructor to develop a written learning plan.
2. Schedule regular supervision.
3. Be prepared for supervision.
4. Seek feedback and evaluation.

5. Seek additional resources and references from your field supervisor.
6. Maintain written documentation of your supervision.

Conclusion

Good field instructor supervision will prepare you for sound professional social work practice grounded in ethics. It teaches about the importance of professional boundaries and the nature of professional relationships. Sound supervision practices in field placement teach how to use supervision in preparing for licensure.

Form a conceptual model of supervision. Find out about the field instructor's model. Pay attention to the structuring of the relationship and the dynamics. Always be sensitive to the ethical considerations that guide the relationship. Given this preparation, you can begin to construct a solid supervisory relationship.

References

National Association of Social Workers. (1996). *Code of Ethics*. Washington, D.C.: Author.

Wininger, B. D. (1995). A social work student's code of ethics. *The New Social Worker, 2* (1), 22-25.

16

Observing Students in the Field

by Ruth T. Weinzettle, MSW, LCSW
and Wendy K. Langley, MSW

Observing Students—From the Educator's View
by Ruth T. Weinzettle, MSW, LCSW

Have you ever asked someone to provide an experience for you that can make your palms sweat, your heart race, and your breathing become difficult? This is exactly what happened approximately three years ago, when the students enrolled in field placement expressed a desire for me to be more involved in their field experience. Specifically, they asked if I could observe them in their field work and give them feedback.

Perhaps I should clarify. I am the Field Coordinator at a small liberal arts private college in central Louisiana. Prior to teaching, I had spent approximately nine years at a family counseling agency and had supervised many clinicians in their work. My distinct impression was that direct observation by a supervisor is a very stressful experience for many people.

When the students made this request, field placement involved two visits every semester by the faculty field coordinator and a two-hour weekly seminar for the students. I was proud of this group of students for being willing to make themselves vulnerable in an effort to learn more about themselves and about social work.

That request began a new venture for me and for the students who have been enrolled in field placements ever since. I have been able to observe students in several different settings and activities. Most commonly, I have observed students facilitating educational and therapeutic groups.

However, I have also read cases, attended staff meetings in which students presented cases, and even attended a hospice visit to a nursing home patient with a student.

I think there are some distinct advantages in having the field coordinator observe the student. First of all, the coordinator gains a better understanding of the agency in several areas, including services offered, clients served, and agency organization.

Direct observation also provides the coordinator an opportunity to assess the student's work and to give feedback. The students, although expressing much fear, usually receive feedback with a sincere interest in improving their skills and becoming more self-aware.

There are also some serious issues that must be considered before an observation occurs. It is always critical that the clients involved are informed about who the coordinator is and his or her purpose in being present, and that they give their consent for the field coordinator's presence. There has never been a situation to date in which a client has declined. Part of that success may be in the choosing of situations that are more appropriate for observations. It is also very important that the coordinator be diplomatic with the agency staff and the agency field supervisor. It must be made clear that the purpose is to assist the student in his or her placement and not necessarily to critique the agency. The agency must always be informed about, and must agree with, the observation plan.

Another issue that needs to be considered is the agreement of the student. Different programs choose to deal with this issue differently. In my program, observation of direct work with a client is not required but is strongly encouraged. However, if observation of direct work cannot occur for any reason, it is requested that the field coordinator review cases or attend staff meetings or other non-direct work. This has seemed to be necessary, because not all settings provide opportunities for observation, and students should not be penalized for this.

Another important consideration is the feedback session with the student. Students very actively seek feedback about every aspect of their work. When I do not give thorough enough feedback, students usually ask until they get what they need. I like to ask the student to critique the experience before I give my feedback. I find that they are often on target with their assessment of the strengths and weaknesses of the situation. It is important to give positive feedback on many points, and I like to give this first. Following this is feedback regarding things that the student might do differently or things that I want to ask him or her to consider. It is always helpful to have specific examples for students. It appears to be more helpful when the feedback addresses the process the student used, as well as the content. The field coordinator might suggest an exercise that the student could use in the future, but other issues are important as well. I particularly look for ways in which the student interacts with the clients and try to draw their attention to their own reactions. For example, I might ask a student if he or she is aware of avoiding a certain person in a group and explore why.

Observation in Action

I would like to discuss one experience in more detail. I made arrangements to observe Wendy, a senior student, in her internship. Wendy was completing her placement at a division of a local hospital that provides educational services to the community. Some of the services the agency provides are school-based health clinics, parenting classes for the general public, grief groups, and self-esteem groups for children and adolescents.

Wendy was leading a group for parents who had been declared abusive or neglectful by the Office of Community Services. The format that she utilized was a program called "Active Parenting," which used a video series and workbooks. I could tell that Wendy was nervous about my being there, but she proceeded to introduce me and to facilitate the group. I observed and took notes, so I could remember to address certain aspects of my feedback with her.

After the group, Wendy and I met to discuss the process. I was very aware of a need to be encouraging and positive, yet give helpful feedback. I asked how she felt about the group, and she stated that the group seemed to interact as they normally would. She had good insight and was able to list the strengths and weaknesses of the group process.

There were many strengths present in the group process. It was obvious that Wendy had established a good rapport with the group. Several had brought pictures of their children to show her, and many went up to talk to her during the break. She also was able to keep the group task-oriented, yet allow some interaction among group members. She also had good examples to make the material more relevant to the group.

One area that concerned me was the level of difficulty of the material presented. (I had noticed that one participant in particular had difficulty writing his name on the name tag.) Since it had been an agency decision to use this program, we worked on the premise that we would not change the program, but rather adjust it to meet the level of understanding of the participants. I had also noted that Wendy made good eye contact with the women in the group and talked to them, but that she avoided the males in the group. This led us into a discussion of gender issues and how this might play out in the group process. We discussed particular exercises that might help everyone in the group to talk, yet stay within the time limits. Wendy was very receptive to the feedback and even seemed energized by it. I thoroughly enjoyed the entire experience and reveled in the supervisor role, which I sometimes miss.

After returning to the college, I did what every good practitioner does and got feedback from my own supervisor, the program director. I relayed the experience to her, and we discussed productive ways to deal with student feedback and diplomatic ways to interact with agencies.

I find that observation is a very rewarding and educational experience for both the student and the field coordinator. When done carefully and with consideration, it is a very positive experience.

■ ■

Being Observed—From the Student's View

by Wendy K. Langley, MSW

Editor's Note: Wendy Langley was a student who was observed by Ruth Weinzettle.

Your palms are sweaty and your heart beats fast. You take deep breaths trying to calm yourself. You're being evaluated by your field coordinator. What makes this such a nerve-wracking experience? Your evaluator is someone you know and trust, and one more person in a group doesn't make that much of a difference. You've been leading the group for a while and have had a chance to become comfortable in the group situation, and yet you feel like a freshman who is just starting out the minute your instructor walks into the room. If you haven't had this experience yet, you probably will at some time during your field placement.

The experience I had with being observed occurred during my field practicum in the community services department of the hospital where I interned. I had been leading a parenting group that was a partnership between the hospital and the Office of Community Support. It was an educational group for parents who were mandated to attend because of abuse or neglect of their children. Some parents had children placed in foster care, while other families remained intact throughout the duration of the group. The group followed a strict curriculum and met once a week for six weeks. It was mainly comprised of females, although there were usually some males in attendance. Also, a caseworker from the Office of Community Support sat in on every class to record attendance, although he or she usually sat in the back of the room and participated minimally in the group.

When my professor and I talked about her coming to observe the group, several thoughts ran through my mind. First, I found it extremely difficult to assert my ability to lead this group. I am young and single, without children, so it was hard for the parents in the group to see me as a valid leader. I did, however, try not to present myself as an expert in parenting, but only as a facilitator for the video-based program. There were also many issues besides parenting to deal with in the group. The fact that some had children in foster care did not make me a welcome face. Some came to the program with anger and resentment toward the Office of Community Support, which was eventually turned toward the group or me. Also, many members of the group had been abused or neglected as children, leading to therapy issues that may have never been addressed; these issues arose in the group when we talked about family of origin parenting. The group's focus, however, was education, and I did not feel competent enough in this area to address the therapy issues.

140 THE FIELD PLACEMENT SURVIVAL GUIDE

Needless to say, with all of these issues going on, I was reluctant to reinforce my student status, as a "practicing" social worker, by introducing my field coordinator. No one likes to know that they are being "practiced" on or to think they are not receiving quality services. I talked with my intern supervisor about how I should introduce my instructor and how I should ask for permission for her to observe. My supervisor reminded me that I was a student and that the clients knew that. The thought of being observed also brought up those feelings of inadequacy that all students experience. Thoughts of "I'm not ready to practice in an agency" ran through my mind once again, as they had before I started my field practicum. Also, I had been verbally attacked the week before by a group member who was angry about her children being taken away, so I was worried about how the group would be this week.

At the start of the group, I introduced my field instructor and explained how I was to be evaluated during the semester to see how I was doing in the agency. No one objected, and they responded in group as they would have if she hadn't been there. I was still aware of my instructor's presence for the first part, but after I relaxed and focused on the group, it was not as bad as I had imagined it would be. After the group, I was able to process with my professor, which was helpful in determining what I could do to improve and what I was doing well already. She also gave me suggestions on ways to handle things differently, such as how to get greater group participation from people who don't always want to be in attendance.

Overall, I found the evaluation process to be helpful. For those who are going to be observed, consider it free advice and support for what you can do to improve your services to clients, since improvement of services is something we as social workers should always be working toward. I would encourage students to be observed by someone non-threatening, such as their field coordinator, who can help direct them in their work for the betterment of their clients.

17

Online Supervision for Social Workers

by Gary S. Stofle, LISW, CCDCIIIE, ACSW,
and Shavone Hamilton, CSW

In September 1997, Shavone Hamilton began a social work internship at Saint Vincent's Westchester in Harrison, New York while in the MSW program at Fordham University. Gary Stofle was assigned as her supervisor. In the first exploratory supervisory sessions, they found out both of them were "online"—they had accounts on America Online (AOL) and they regularly signed onto the service and communicated with others through chat rooms and e-mail. In addition, Gary had been providing online psychotherapy since December 1996 with a client in a chat room on AOL.

As they began to decide upon scheduling supervisory sessions, they discussed the possibility of conducting some supervisory sessions online. They both found the idea convenient, because they each spent a certain amount of time each day online. They also found the idea exciting, because no current literature in social work or psychology explored an interactive, chat room model of supervision. They wanted to add to the social work knowledge base by seeing if supervision conducted online could work. Shavone sought and was granted permission from Fordham University for one hour face-to-face supervision and one hour online supervision each week. They began their online work on October 7, 1997, and met weekly online until May 1998, when Shavone completed the MSW program. The following is their account of this experience.

The Process of Online Supervision

Options included in America Online make it quite easy to conduct online supervision. AOL has an option called "Buddy List," which can easily be edited to include the screen name of any other AOL member. We added each other's name to our Buddy Lists and so knew when the other was online. We would sign onto the service at the scheduled time. Gary would send an instant message (IM) to Shavone and ask if she was ready to start supervision. Shavone would reply in the affirmative, and Gary would send her an invitation to a chat room to begin the supervision (chat room invitations are another option on the Buddy List). We simply clicked the "go" button and we both would be in the same private chat room.

Once in the chat room, we started the work. As in face-to-face supervision, we exchanged pleasantries and then decided on the focus of the supervision session. Gary generally asked Shavone where she wanted to start and we went from there. Shavone provided process recordings weekly, and those were often the focus of the supervision, both face-to-face and online. At other times, situations would occur that were not the subject of a process, but deserved immediate attention, and we would focus on those situations. We identified clients only by their initials, in order to preserve confidentiality (which will be discussed in more detail later).

In addition to our scheduled online supervision sessions in real time, we sent e-mail back and forth regarding work assignments, clients, and other issues. We maintained confidentiality in e-mail in the same way we did in the chat room—using only initials and no identifying information.

Requirements for Effective Online Supervision

In order to derive the maximum benefit from the process of online supervision, both the supervisor and student should meet certain criteria:

- Have skill in navigating online.
- Have basic typing and spelling skills.
- Be able to express self in the written word.
- Be able to express concepts/ideas without the use of non-verbal cues.
- Have excellent communication skills.

Basic skill in online navigation is quite easy to learn and master. AOL has devised the Buddy List to be user friendly, and in a relatively short period of time a person with at least some computer background can set up online supervision.

Each participant in this process needs basic typing and spelling skills—neither of which can be quickly and easily learned if you don't already possess these skills. Since text is the means of communication, if you must spend minutes physically typing out a response, the flow of the communication changes and could be misinterpreted as being distracted by outside elements or as a non-response. If you misspell words, your communication can have an entirely different meaning from what you intended. With the absence of the non-verbal cues, the potential for miscommunication is great and can have quite an impact on this process.

The participants in this process need to be able to express themselves well through the written word. What we've found is that it's not so much that you have to communicate in complete sentences; it's that you have to choose words that get the meaning you want across in the most clear and succinct manner possible.

Online interaction does not allow for the use of non-verbal cues. Many of us use our hands, voice intonation, and so on to provide important components of our communication. Online, adjustments have to be made to take into account the limitations of text-only communication. On the other hand, abbreviations and certain characters that are quite succinct can powerfully express feelings and add tone to the communication. Examples of some of these characters are listed below:

:)	Smile
<g>	Grin
:(	Frown
;)	Wink
:P	Disappointed
:O	Shocked
?	What?/Explain/Why?
BTW	By The Way
BRB	Be Right Back
LOL	Laugh Out Loud
OTOH	On The Other Hand
SO	Significant Other
TTYL	Talk To You Later

Confidentiality

In the chat rooms on AOL, there is a text box on the screen that shows the viewer all people who are in the chat room. This is an important feature and helps make online discussions secure. What is said in a chat room is not recorded by AOL; however, the discussion can be recorded by participants in the chat using the "logging" feature (another option on AOL). In spite of the security that comes from knowing no other people are in the room with us, we decided to identify clients only by initials. Of course, we both knew which clients were assigned to Shavone, so it was not a problem when Shavone would say, "I need to talk about my individual session with G. today." We were able to talk meaningfully and in depth about this client without revealing any demographic data.

We also communicated via e-mail about clients, events that occurred while Gary was on vacation, and other significant practice/supervision issues that arose between supervision periods. Initials only were used to identify clients when sending e-mail. We found that using initials to identify clients via e-mail protected confidentiality. Additionally, each member account on AOL can be accessed only with a password. Also, AOL allows for "preferences" regarding e-mail. Individuals can choose not to save e-mail in the archives AOL offers for each account. Choosing to save e-mail in archives makes old e-mail messages available on the computer's hard drive without a password, unless they are saved in a program like Word 97, which has a password protection feature for any file.

Online Boundaries

Privacy and boundaries can emerge as issues for those involved in online supervision. The use of Buddy Lists on AOL lets anyone who has your screen name know when you are online. The Instant Message feature allows one person to send a message to another person in real time without the sender knowing if the receiver is involved in another activity online. This was not a problem for us during our online supervision, probably because of the respect we have for one another. It is conceivable that boundary issues or violations can occur in an online supervisory relationship. Both the supervisor and the student simply need to set appropriate limits and express their level of comfort regarding instant messages at times other than scheduled supervision.

Disadvantages/Advantages

Some disadvantages to providing supervision online are noted below:

- *Lack of non-verbal cues.* We depend, at least in part, on the sum of all the person's reactions, including all the cues that are non-verbal. It takes some getting used to in relying only on the written word and certain characters to express feelings.
- *Technical problems with the online process.* Busy signals may prevent one from signing on to the Internet, or the network may be slow, for example.
- *Typing*—if either supervisor or supervisee has problems with typing, this can slow the process down and make it uncomfortable.
- *Space limitations*—if the message is particularly detailed, it can't be sent all at once and the other person can respond to only part of the message.
- *Silence/inactivity* between typed sentences can be interpreted as the other being distracted or not paying attention, instead of thoughtful or respectful silence.
- *Distractions*—if you are typing at home, your spouse or other family members can be unaware that you are in the middle of a supervision session and seek your attention.

The advantages to online supervision are noted below:

- *Simplicity*—online supervision is a simple and straightforward process for those who are familiar with online navigation and who have good typing skills.
- *Convenience*—supervision is done in the comfort of one's home or office. No travel is involved.
- *Ease of expression*—some issues are easier to express online as opposed to face-to-face. An example noted by Shavone was discussing countertransferential issues

online. Shavone discussed the feelings that were brought up in her related to a client who was having a particularly difficult time staying sober over the Christmas holidays. As she said, "Some things are easier to write than to say."

- *Permanency*—each can keep a permanent record of the entire supervisory session. This can be used as a reference in regard to information given in the session or with any follow-up that is needed.

Reactions

Shavone: This form of supervision was appealing and easy to adapt to because of my familiarity with AOL's online service and options. Another aspect that made this process work was the face-to-face supervisory relationship. The pre-existing supervisory relationship created a comfortable atmosphere in the online process.

When Gary offered feedback and learning material, I had references from face-to-face sessions that helped with any potential misunderstandings of content. I knew how to interpret his suggestions from previous face-to-face supervision.

Online sessions were just as productive as face-to-face sessions. Lack of non-verbal communication cues made the expression of certain emotions difficult, but where non-verbal cues were needed, words were substituted. For example, if I was having difficulty expressing a complicated situation for a client during face-to-face supervision, Gary would take notice of my facial expression, my posture, or a gesture I made with my hands and try to help me focus the presentation. However, during online supervision, this was not possible. If there was difficulty with expression, this had to be written in order for the other party to know of the difficulty. If I was confused about a particular suggestion, I typed a message asking for clarification. If I agreed with a suggestion, instead of nodding, as I would do in person, I wrote "yes" or "right."

Finally, material gained from face-to-face sessions is often invaluable. Yet, soon after supervision, one may not be able to recall the suggestions and/or recommended model(s) for intervention. Online supervision eliminates this dilemma with its recording option.

Gary: I saw the potential for online supervision as a natural outgrowth of my work online with a client. In this online psychotherapy, I saw that I could establish a relationship, teach, role model, and help the client develop self awareness using only text. If psychotherapy could be done in a chat room, then surely supervision could be done as well.

I have supervised a number of MSW students since 1989, all of whom were supervised face-to-face. All of these students were able to learn skills in helping clients, to increase their understanding of chemical dependency and its treatment, and to learn more about themselves as helpers, especially how they are affected on a feelings level by this work. Shavone, the first student I've supervised online, was able to learn and accomplish in all of these areas as well through a combination of face-to-face and online supervision.

While we utilized face-to-face to establish the supervisor and student relationship, the relationship was deepened during our online supervisory sessions. It was deepened through Shavone's increased openness online regarding certain issues, particularly countertransference. As she felt more comfortable opening up online, I got to know more about her as a student and a worker, which moved our work together further along.

Our face-to-face interactions were duplicated online in the sense of style of communication, tone, words used, and tempo. I did not see online work as limiting the issues/topics we could discuss.

For teaching, online supervision is ideal in the sense that the student has a verbatim record of the teaching that can be referred to in the future. A technique I call "Segmented Biblioteaching" can be used in online supervision. This technique is described below:

1. The student asks a question or presents an issue from a process recording that stimulates the supervisor to provide specific information or teaching.
2. The supervisor types a segment of a teaching (such as affect management or cognitive behavioral therapy) that directly addresses the student's question/issue.
3. The supervisor and student discuss the teaching and how it applies specifically to the situation, and what changes may be needed on the part of the student or other interventions that can be implemented in the future.

This process (and online supervision, in general) requires the supervisor to be knowledgeable about a variety of interventions and theories, and to have a good sense of what a student needs to know in various situations with the population being served by the agency. It is very important that the supervisor be experienced enough to be able to "fill in the blanks." By that, I mean the supervisor needs to be able to recognize themes from what the student is typing and respond to those themes. If the supervisor can quickly understand the issues being presented because of his or her clinical experience, the student feels understood and the online communication process is enhanced.

Summary and Implications

The essential components of supervision in social work— establishing a relationship between supervisor and student, teaching, modeling, discussing feelings, managing countertransference, and skill building—can all be completed in online supervision. The supervisor and student both need to have some degree of comfort navigating online and be able to communicate accurately through the typewritten word in order to make this process work. In addition, the supervisor needs to be experienced in supervision in order to be able to function as a supervisor without the visual cues available in face-to-face interactions.

It is clear that online supervision can easily be an adjunct to face-to-face supervision for social work students. Gary plans to continue providing online supervision to MSW students in the future.

Online supervision can possibly replace ongoing face-to-face supervision if the need exists, such as when the supervisor and student are separated by a great distance. It is recommended to begin any online supervision with sufficient face-to-face supervision in order that both the supervisor and the student attain some degree of comfort with one another. As is said in much of the literature about supervision, the relationship is the thing. If a solid, trusting relationship can be established between the supervisor and the student, and both are motivated to participate in online supervision, then it can work.

For Further Reading

Fox, R. (1989). Relationship: The cornerstone of clinical supervision. *The Journal of Contemporary Social Work, 70(3),* 146-152.

Keller, J. F., Protinsky, H. O., Lichtman, M., and Allen, K. (1996). The process of clinical supervision: Direct observation research. *The Clinical Supervisor, 14(1),* 51-63.

Lowey, L. (1983). Social work supervision: From models toward theory. *Journal of Education for Social Work, 19* (2), 55-62.

Rich, P. (1993). The form, function, and content of clinical supervision: An integrated model. *The Clinical Supervisor, 11* (1), 137-178.

Ross, J. (1992). Clinical supervision: Key to effective social work. *Health and Social Work, 17* (2), 83-85.

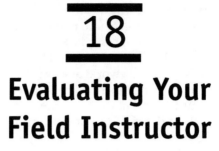

18

Evaluating Your Field Instructor

by Charles E. Floyd, Ph.D., LCSW

It's nearing the end of the school year and your school is asking you to evaluate your field instructor's performance. You notice some pangs of anxiety, because you feel somewhat uncomfortable about shifting into the role of the evaluator. And, as you reflect back, you wonder how you might evaluate some of those behaviors you found a little difficult to accept. After all, your field instructor is a professional social worker in an agency in the community where you plan to work.

Sound familiar? About 90% of schools of social work rely on students to evaluate their field instructors. It is a convenient way for schools to get some feedback on field instructors' performance. Many field coordinators know of few alternatives to get evaluative data on their field instructors. In many cases, faculty liaisons may know very little about field instructors' performance. A school's routine contact with its field instructors may be quite limited. As a result, many schools depend almost solely on their students for evaluations.

Field coordinators need information on field instructors' performance for several reasons. It helps them to identify the best way to use field instructors, to identify training needs, and plan field instructor development programs. It also helps field programs identify problems and take action. Schools evaluate for different reasons and use the information in different ways.

It helps if you know why your school evaluates its field instructors and how it intends to use the evaluative information. Your first step is to find out about the evaluation process by asking your field coordinator or your faculty liaison to explain the purpose of the evaluation and how the field program plans to use the information. Knowing this will help you understand the evaluation process and support your role in evaluating. Some research studies suggest that students are less apt to complete evaluations if they are unclear about how the information will be used.

Many schools of social work ask students to evaluate their field instructors once during the academic year. Usually, this comes at the end of the placement. As a result, you may find yourself in the position of evaluating your field instructor for the first time just as you prepare to terminate your placement. End-of-the-year evaluations may be helpful to your school in determining field instructor overall performance, but they may do little in contributing to your field instructor's development. End-of-the-year evaluations are considered summative evaluations and are commonly used for administrative purposes. They provide a global measure of how your field instructor is doing his or her job. In other words, they give the field coordinator some idea about how well he or she is providing field instruction. As a rule, they do little to promote professional development.

You will have some biases. Several variables may influence your evaluation without your being aware of them. Because of certain biases and influences, some field programs may be skeptical about the accuracy of student evaluations. Skepticism about the accuracy of student evaluations may determine whether the field program uses the results. Every evaluation process should consider possible biases when interpreting the results.

The first step is for you to be aware of what might potentially influence your evaluation. Whether you are a first-year or second-year student can influence your evaluation. Some studies suggest that first-year students are more apt to be critical of field instructors. The quality of your relationship with your field instructor can bias your overall evaluation. For obvious reasons, you may be more likely to give high ratings to your field instructor's performance if you have a close positive relationship. This is understandable, but it is an example of a biased evaluation. Be aware that your emotional state and your grade expectations may bias your evaluation. To minimize their influence, consider the timing of the evaluation.

One major concern influencing student evaluations is the lack of anonymity. Some studies suggest that students fear negative repercussions from their field instructors if the evaluation is negative. The typical one-to-one relationship often makes students feel more vulnerable. Consider this factor when you evaluate your field instructor. How do you think this will affect your attitude toward evaluating his or her performance? Will your fear of possible repercussions affect your honesty in rating your field instructor's performance?

Who Gets the Information?

Evaluative information generally goes to the field coordinator, and many times that is where it remains. A minority of schools share the information with their field instructors. In part, this is due to the belief that the accuracy of the evaluations might go down, because students are fearful of backlash from field instructors who get negative evaluations. Also, some research shows that it takes at least fifteen students to accurately evaluate teaching performance. One student's rating of a field instructor may not be very reliable. Some schools make this information available to incoming students, thinking that the information might help them make decisions about placements.

It can help if you know who has access to your evaluation and how it might be used. If your school does not share the information with the field instructor, are you expected to do this? As odd as it might seem, many field instructors never see their evaluations. Some schools consider the information useful for several administrative reasons, but not necessarily appropriate for use by the field instructor. There is some validity to this thinking if you realize that some evaluative instruments provide little more than global information about performance and say little about specific performance behaviors. Global information does little in promoting field instructors' skills, but it may help your school get a general idea about performance.

Is Your Evaluation Considered Confidential?

Find out whether the information is considered confidential and, if so, if it is protected in a manner to assure confidentiality. This may make a difference in how comfortable you feel in participating in the evaluation.

Evaluating someone in the profession brings with it some ethical obligations. Know what your ethical obligations are to the field instructor. In some schools, field instructors may be unaware of being evaluated. The NASW *Code of Ethics* addresses the issue of performance evaluations. Subsection 3.03 describes the ethical obligations pertaining to performance evaluations. Subsection 3.03 states that social workers need to carry out evaluations in a "fair and considerate manner on the basis of clearly stated criteria." Carry out your evaluation of your field instructor with this ethical responsibility in mind. Take the evaluation seriously and value its importance.

So What Happens Next?

Anticipate that your social work department will provide you with a questionnaire to rate your field instructor's performance. Questionnaires vary in design, but generally they might include several specific performance items, global performance items using Likert ratings, and open-ended items that ask for narrative comment. Review the form and familiarize yourself with the school's procedures for conducting the evaluation.

Ask yourself if you understand the purpose of the evaluation. Recognize that, in principle, the primary purpose of evaluating is to promote and foster your field instructor's professional development. It helps if you evaluate their performance in the spirit of helping them become better at field instruction. It also helps to realize that going through an evaluation process can be difficult for field instructors—if they are aware of the evaluation. Like you, they want helpful feedback on how they did and what changes they may need to consider to improve performance. If possible, don't wait until the last day to evaluate your field instructor. Several schools use a procedure in which, at the end of their placements, students fill out a questionnaire independent of dialogue with the field instructor. The completed form often goes directly to the coordinator. For a meaningful and more effective evaluation, consider using the following option.

As part of your professional relationship with your field instructor, make it a point to routinely give feedback on his or her performance. You may want to formally state this in your learning contract. This kind of learning experience can tie in quite nicely with your goal of understanding and using supervision. To identify specific performance behaviors, familiarize yourself with the performance items used in the school's questionnaire. To supplement these items, ask your field instructor to suggest some performance measures. Add some of your measures. The point is for you to get an idea of relevant performance measures that will enable you to provide appropriate feedback.

Feedback needs to be direct, honest, and in the spirit of helping one improve. And it needs to be timely. Providing feedback to your field instructor requires a solid working relationship built on trust, mutual respect, and good communication. If you feel resistant to the idea of giving your field instructor feedback, examine what this may mean about the nature of your working relationship. Providing feedback on one's performance is a working part of professional relationships. Think of evaluating and giving feedback as a maintenance activity in the educational experience. Ignored, the quality of the relationship suffers. As the quality of the relationship suffers, so may the educational experience.

Schools of social work are aware that evaluating field instructors is not easy and that there are several problems with reliability. End-of-the-year evaluative measures give broad brush images of performance. Your decision to routinely provide performance feedback on specific behaviors can be one very meaningful way for your field instructor to improve.

At the end of your placement, when you sit down to fill out the formal performance evaluation, ask your field instructor to participate. If you have been providing feedback all along, it should be relatively easy to complete the school's formal questionnaire. There should be no surprises.

As an intern, you are learning what it means to be a professional. As an intern evaluating your field instructor, you are learning good supervision behaviors guided by ethical responsibilities.

PART V

OFF AND RUNNING

PART V: OFF AND RUNNING

Think of the field placement as a marathon. You've trained thoroughly, you've done as much advance preparation as you can, and now you're off and running. You will reach the finish line when you have successfully accomplished the goals set forth in your learning plan.

You are ready to put into action the theories and skills you have learned in the classroom. How will you know when you have successfully mastered these skills? Some signs include:

- development of "good" professional habits
- recognition and elimination of "bad" habits
- understanding what constitutes a successful beginning and ending with clients
- possessing a genuine, deep comprehension of ethical issues and the decision-making process that is necessary to practice social work ethically
- knowing the connection between social justice/advocacy and practice

Much of your learning now will be from your experience—with clients, with a supervisor, and with an agency—coupled with the self-examination that is part of the supervision and learning process.

This section provides some tools to help you along the way.

19

Good Habits for Practicum Students

by Julie Birkenmaier, MSW, LCSW,
and Marla Berg-Weger, Ph.D.

"Alex"

Alex's first practicum in a hospital did not go well. He had always followed instructions well at his previous jobs and received high praise. However, he felt unprepared for his first professional experience. Alex completed all the work given to him and thought that he had done everything well. He did not think that arriving a few minutes late, leaving a few minutes early on occasion, completing homework assignments when not busy with practicum activities, and taking several sick days were problems, because he had always informed his field instructor.

However, his field instructor gave him a mediocre evaluation at the mid-practicum site visit and for the final evaluation. He heard himself described with phrases such as "needs more initiative," "floundering," and "unreliable." After consulting with his faculty field liaison, he decided to take a much different approach to his second practicum.

For his next practicum at a community mental health facility, he familiarized himself with agency materials prior to the start of the practicum and arrived the first day ready to observe staff conducting intakes and assessments. He made sure to arrive ten minutes early every day and never left early, even if it meant that he had to pursue assignments from other staff. He only took one day off to attend a friend's wedding that had been arranged before the practicum began. He worked hard to get his assignments completed in a timely manner, and he asked his field instructor for an extra project. With the help of his research professor, he re-designed the evaluation form for a group he facilitated and piloted the use of the tool during his practicum. Based on his initial use of the tool and the feedback received, he revised the instrument and left notes for the staff member who took over facilitating the group. The evaluation from this experience was glowing, and included such phrases as "a valuable asset to the organization," "demonstrates a high degree of professionalism," and "great promise for the profession."

Good Habits and Your Reputation

Practica experiences are opportunities to gain new skills and test waters for your professional career as a social worker. As the scenario with "Alex" demonstrates, the transition from non-professional to a professional position can be difficult. While your university-based and agency-based instructors may assist you with obtaining placements, arranging learning experiences, and fulfilling the practicum requirements of your program, what type of approach and personal habits are going to serve you well in your field placement? If field placements are to be a training ground for your practice after graduation, implementation of "good habits" in your placement will serve to maximize your learning experiences and ingrain good habits that you can carry with you into your post-graduation practice.

The practicum experience can be the mechanism used by students to begin building a professional reputation. Your practicum experience can allow you to network with other professionals in a practice area, both in and outside of the practicum agency. The resulting relationships can be the foundation of your employment searches in the future (Webb, 1999). What makes for effective practica experiences that will assist you to build a positive professional reputation? The following are suggestions that, if adopted, can increase your effectiveness in your practicum.

1. Hit The Ground Running.

Ideally, you should do some background research on the agency when you interview for the site, and be familiar with the mission, services, and demographics of the clients served by the agency. If you have not done so in advance, be sure to gather this information at the very beginning of the practicum experience. When possible, talk to other students who have completed a placement or are currently placed at the agency to gather information about the function and roles of the staff members. You may obtain agency materials, such as policy and procedure manuals, prior to your first day, so you can familiarize yourself with policies and procedures before you arrive. Assure your field instructor that you are eager to contribute to the work of the agency as soon as possible, and ask about observing other staff members from the beginning. Ask about the timing of beginning to work with clients under close supervision. Make it clear that you would like to contribute to the agency as a team player as quickly as possible and that you are willing to work hard to do so.

2. Assume Responsibility For Your Own Learning.

The field instructor, student, and faculty field liaison work together to develop a satisfactory learning experience for the practicum. However, the practicum is often much less structured than a course, and you would benefit from viewing the practicum as a process rather than as a product. Seek out learning opportunities that will challenge you. If opportunities are not presented, you may need to create opportunities for new responsibilities. Ideally, your field instructor and faculty field liaison will assist you to make the transition from being a passive learner to an active professional (Royse, Dhooper, & Rompf, 1996). Being proactive about your learning experiences can empower you to take responsibility for obtaining the type of experiences you are seeking. For example, look for opportunities to attend relevant workshops and in-service training opportunities, facilitate staff or committee meetings, or take on extra assignments.

3. Seek Opportunities to Go Beyond Expectations (Yours as Well as Others).

Do you know what your expectations are for this experience? Your field instructor's? Clearly, reasonable expectations for roles and responsibilities, as well as level of performance, vary widely depending upon the agency, program, and level of experience. When possible, articulate your expectations for your performance in the practicum, and ask your field instructor to do the same. Set high goals for yourself. Is it possible that you would be able to write an entire grant rather than parts of a grant? Could you testify by yourself before a legislative body? Can you facilitate a group meeting without your field instructor (or another staff member) in the room? Can you serve as a client's primary therapist? Often, higher expectations will involve more effort and the risk of failure, but your student status should encourage you to take appropriate risks and see "failure" as a learning experience. Should you fail when attempting an activity, your field instructor, other staff, and faculty field liaison can provide constructive feedback and support.

4. Manage Your Time Effectively.

Time is often a scarce resource for students. You may be earning your social work degree while juggling a job and family responsibilities. When possible, seek to establish a reasonable schedule that you can maintain for your practicum over the course of the semester or year, even if it means temporarily sacrificing other areas of your life (such as time with friends and family, "down" time relaxing, and so forth). A practicum should take more time than a course, so budgeting your time carefully is essential to both your well-being and your effectiveness in practicum. Try to work on assignments in advance of due dates to avoid completing assignments at the last minute.

5. Clarify and Abide By Expectations for Professional Behavior.

Professional behavior includes such areas as work ethic, relationships, and responsibilities with co-workers and clients, and representation of the agency to the community. Students often experience higher expectations of work-related behavior when transitioning from non-professional to professional responsibilities (Ross, 1997). For example, students may have experienced employment situations in the past in which friends and family could make brief visits while working, personal calls were acceptable, the completion of homework was allowed, arriving a few minutes late or leaving a few minutes early was common, uniforms were worn, sick time was taken liberally, and engagement in organizational politics was the norm. A professional practicum experience will likely include more responsibility and higher expectations about work-related behavior. With your field instructor, clarify expectations regarding such issues as:

- time spent at work (Are personal calls allowed from the agency? Can you run errands during lunch time?)
- dress expectations (What are the agency dress code policies? Are Fridays casual dress days?)
- expectations around sick and vacation time
- the importance of timeliness (What should you do if you must arrive late or leave early?)

Additionally, ask about key players in the organization and seek to avoid office politics whenever possible (Webb, 1999).

6. Actively Pursue Your Learning Goals.

While you might not be able to define all of your learning activities, seek to gain experience in the areas in which you wish to attain skills and knowledge. While some flexibility will enable you to pursue unexpected learning opportunities as they arise, being focused will help you to maximize your learning. Stephen Covey, in his book *The Seven Habits of Highly Effective People* (1989) describes the principle of "beginning with the end in mind" (p. 98). He states that a truly effective person "starts with a clear understanding of your destination...so that the steps you take are always in the right direction."

Unless you have an idea of the skills, knowledge, and experience you think will assist you in your long-term plans, you might be very busy in practicum, but not engaged in learning the skills and knowledge most valuable to you. If you decide to change your goals as you move through your practica experiences, you can change your focus. Commitment to this habit will involve a high degree of investment at the beginning of your practicum in crafting an accurate and detailed learning agreement, as well as monitoring the completion of activities throughout the semester.

7. Leave a Legacy for the Agency.

Look for opportunities to leave your mark on the agency after you have completed your practicum. Completing a product or resource needed by the organization or organizing a process demonstrates that you can take initiative and have the drive that can ensure your positive reputation at the agency and, more than likely, in the field of practice in the area (Berg-Weger & Birkenmaier, 2000). You might ask your field instructor about where the most attention is needed in the program or organization and offer your help in undertaking an unfinished project.

Examples of a legacy include: setting up a new computer software program and training the other staff, attending a workshop and presenting an in-service on the material to the staff, re-organizing and updating a resource manual, designing and piloting an evaluation instrument for group work, designing a Web page for the organization or program, or organizing a manual for future student interns.

Conclusion

The practica experiences are a crucial component of your social work education. Implementing these effective habits in your practica can involve a great deal of energy, commitment and time. However, this investment can serve to maximize your learning and satisfaction with the experiences, as well as enhance your professional reputation in the field.

References

Berg-Weger, M., & Birkenmaier, J. M. (2000). *The practicum companion for social work: Integrating class and field work.* Boston: Allyn & Bacon.

Covey, S. R. (1989). *The seven habits of highly effective people.* New York: Simon & Schuster.

Ross, S. T. (1997). A building block to your career. *The New Social Worker, 4* (1), 16–17.

Royse, D., Dhooper, S. S., & Rompf, E. L. (1996). *Field instruction: A guide for social work students* (2nd ed.). White Plains, NY: Longman.

Webb, A. (1999). 10 tips for the transition from field placement to employment. *The New Social Worker, 6* (4), 4–5.

20

Eliminating Bad Habits in the Social Work Interview

by Don Collins, Ph.D., MSW, BSW
and Heather Coleman, Ph.D., MSW, BSW

"Dysfunctional" interviewing behaviors sometimes arise in the interactions between a novice social worker and a client. They are considered dysfunctional because they have a negative impact on the relationship and can create barriers to goal attainment. Dysfunctional interviewing behaviors are "bad habits" that can be replaced with functional skills (Collins, 1990). Both relationship-building skills and bad habits can be identified in transcripts. Failing to communicate a thought clearly has the same outcome in writing and interviewing in that recipients are baffled by the message, and the intent of a message is often buried under needless words and behaviors.

In an early study of the transfer of interviewing skills from the classroom to the field, Collins (1984) noted a significant drop in core conditions from an interviewing laboratory to the field. A later study (Collins, 1990) revealed that the core conditions (empathy, warmth, and genuineness) were replaced by dysfunctional questioning behaviors. The increase in dysfunctional behaviors partly accounted for the failure to transfer skills from a role-play to the field.

One example stands out in this study. A student asked: "What concerns bring you here today?" The client responded: "I am feeling so overwhelmed with sadness as my mother just died. I was very close to my mother. I just don't know what to do. In particular, I don't know how to tell my kids, as they were very close to their grandmother" (Collins, 1990). Had this been a role-play, the student would probably have responded along the lines of: "I am so sorry to hear about the loss of your mother. Not only is it hard for you to deal with your feelings about her loss, it sounds as if you are finding it difficult to know how to explain her death to your children." This statement contains warmth and reflection, and demonstrates caring and understanding. In reality, the student responded to the client by saying: "How old did you say your children were?" The student did not demonstrate warmth or understanding, which would have been very helpful at this beginning point. Instead, the student asked a closed-ended question, which was problematic at this stage of the interview. Later, the question of the age of the children may have been more appropriate.

One explanation for this lapse is that the student became anxious with a real client and reverted to "bad habits." Another explanation is that in the classroom, students practice primarily with YAVIS (Young, Attractive, Verbal, Intelligent, and Successful) "clients." From this, we conclude that useful learning should involve classroom experiences typical of clients in field practica. It is important that classroom experiences connect with what students encounter elsewhere.

"Bad Habits"

"Bad habits" fall into four categories: distracting behaviors, pacing, quality of the interview, and communication barriers (Anstey, Bradford, & Yumol, 1998). They are "habits" because the interviewer is not using them intentionally, nor do they target a specific client response. Many arise from interviewer anxiety and serve to reduce interviewer discomfort in times of uncertainty. Figure 1 lists possible "bad habits" that can detract from an interview.

Distracting Behaviors

The first distracting behavior is the verbal utterance that often appears when a social worker is learning to interview. Some common utterances include: "right," "sure," "uh-huh," and "okay." An utterance typically appears in reaction to what a client is saying. There are two kinds of utterances. The first includes those not attached to any other communication:

Figure 1—List of Bad Habits

- Excessive utterances, excessive head nodding
- "Why" Questions
- Use of poor grammar—use of "That" and "It"
- Closed Questions
- Talking more than clients talk
- Machine gun questioning in the form of a series of closed questioning that resembles grilling
- Leading questions
- Placating
- Minimizing
- Rescuing
- Fidgeting
- Poor attending skills
- Giggling at inappropriate parts of the interview or during silences
- Use of repetitive words such as "You know," "like," "okay," "uh huh"
- Advice giving
- Multiple, double barreled questions
- Slouching
- Letting the client ramble
- Taking on cultural traits/language/client specific behaviors that are "phony"
- Taking sides with clients
- Giving false reassurance or agreement when inappropriate
- Ignoring cues about the client's subjective experience of the problem while dealing exclusively with "objective" material
- Judgmental responding
- Inappropriate use of humor or other responses to threatening areas that inhibit discussion or undermine trust
- Premature problem solving
- Criticizing or belittling clients and condescending behaviors
- Over-reliance on "chit-chat"
- Overprotecting clients by avoiding clear cues to implicit information

e.g.: CLIENT: "My husband wants to leave me and..."
SOCIAL WORKER: "Uh-huh."

The second kind of utterance prefaces a statement:

e.g.: CLIENT: "My husband is going to leave and I'm really upset. I don't know what to do."
SOCIAL WORKER: "Uh-huh. Did he say when he would be leaving?"

A more appropriate response to the first kind of utterance would be to tell the client what is meant by "uh-huh," such as, "Tell me more about...." The utterance alone is not helpful; a better response would be direct, clear, and reflective. The question also needs to be asked whether the utterance was intentional, and if so, what was the intention. Utterances such as this are a security blanket for new interviewers. While many texts reinforce the use of utterances, most also make it clear that the intent of an utterance is to encourage the client to speak. However, novices often use utterances with no purpose, even with verbal clients who need no encouragement. And, when utterances appear forty or fifty times in a 10-minute segment of an interview, purposefulness is difficult to accept. Further, most utterances do not convince that the social worker is listening to the client, because it is possible to "fake" an interview with excessive utterances.

The second kind of utterance is not as problematic as the first. Nevertheless, it is still more effective to tell the client exactly what the interviewer means. The statement after an utterance typically should be a response or reflection to model clear, open, honest, and direct communication in the hope that the client will also communicate likewise.

Utterances can also be dangerous by sending the wrong message.

e.g.: CLIENT: "I hit my wife last night!"
SOCIAL WORKER: "Okay."

Although the social worker is trying to encourage the client to continue talking, the client could interpret "okay" as acceptance of the abusive behavior. The most effective way to stop utterances is to use reflections and accurate responding. Reflecting in a clear and warm manner allows the client to feel validated and strengthens the relationship. Non-verbal utterances can also be distracting. Non-verbal communication is powerful and makes up eighty percent of all communication.

Non-verbal communication includes two areas: proxemics and kinesics. Proxemics deals with the physical or personal space between a social worker and a client. Physical distance involves the closeness of the social worker and client. Sitting too close may threaten clients or make them feel invaded, whereas sitting too far may appear as disinterest or coldness. A meaningful distance must be negotiated based on culture, gender, and client discomfort. Warmth can be conveyed non-verbally through such behaviors as leaning toward and turning toward the client, sitting in a relaxed position, maintaining eye contact, and smiling (Lishman, 1994).

The comfort level in the relationship concerns the degree of personal closeness. It varies among clients depending on many variables, such as gender, ethnicity, how well the client knows the social worker, and if the client likes the social worker. These can affect whether the social worker and the client have a good relationship. Proxemics also includes posture. Usually, if the social worker adopts a relaxed and open posture, the client will feel as if the social worker is warm and genuinely interested. However, client perceptions about whether the social worker's posture is too relaxed (uninvolved) or, alternatively, too rigid (disapproving or tense) can be distracting.

Kinesics is the second type of non-verbal behavior and includes eye contact, facial expressions, body movements, and gestures. Eye contact is important to convey that the social worker is attentive and interested. The social worker needs to make sufficient eye contact to ensure that clients do not feel as though they are not being heard. If eye contact is intense, it may feel as if the social worker is staring or being intrusive. Again, the social worker needs to find a balance. Variables such as culture or gender may also play a role. For example, in some cultures, direct eye contact is a sign of disrespect.

Clients will read feelings and attitudes into facial expressions. Facial expressions must be congruent with verbal communication. For example, the client may interpret frowning

as criticism, when it may be that the social worker is confused. Exaggerated or excessive facial expressions can be
distracting, because clients may think that the social worker
is having trouble concentrating or is feeling uncomfortable.

Distracting body movements and gestures include stiff-
ness or jerky movements during an interview, which can not
only distract the client, but affect the relationship, since the
client may think the social worker is feeling uncomfortable.
Head nodding is a common interviewing gesture. The social
worker, often unknowingly, head nods, signaling to the client to keep talking. Head nodding conveys that the behavior
is appropriate. In reality, the social worker means "Tell me
more." Yet, sometimes the client has already shared information, and a reflective response would be more appropriate. Together with the use of "uh huh," head nods are the
most frequent unintentional interviewing behavior. It is not
uncommon to count up to seventy head nods and "uh huhs"
in a ten-minute interviewing segment.

If the client has conveyed information, it is probably difficult to keep track of all the themes. It would be more effective to listen to a few minutes of information and then reflect
or summarize. This also tells clients that they are heard.

Gestures such as preening, hair twirling, pen tapping,
and foot jerking can rob attention from the interaction. The
social worker needs to become aware of these and other behaviors because of how clients can interpret them. Body
movements and gestures can also enhance communication,
but they must fit the topic and not distract. The social worker
must learn effective ways of communicating to make behavior and communication congruent. Once these skills are mastered, relationship building becomes easier.

Pacing the Interview

Pacing refers to the rate of speech and the frequency of
turn taking (Gorden, 1992). Indeed, in most initial interviews, it is appropriate for the client to talk as much as eighty
percent. Effective pacing can be undermined by several behaviors, including excessive questioning, irrelevant and
closed-ended questions, limited use of silence, and speed of
the interviewer's speech.

The style of the questioning influences the pace. Excessive questioning creates a tense atmosphere resembling in-

terrogation. It is crucial for the client to feel at ease and comfortable, and to openly discuss experiences. Questions should be limited to no more than two consecutively, punctuated with silence or reflection. Excessive questioning will shut the client down, create anxiety, and decrease the chance of obtaining relevant information.

Irrelevant and closed-ended questions also erect barriers. The social worker must remain focused, because an irrelevant line of questioning will serve no purpose and key client information will be ignored or minimized. Irrelevant questions are also frustrating and give the impression that the client is not being taken seriously.

Pacing can also be affected by incoherent questioning (questions that do not relate to one another) or a loss of thoughts. If the social worker fails to respond to the client, the client may feel unheard, invalidated, and doubting the social worker's effectiveness. Similarly, closed-ended questions limit the scope of the information obtained, and corners the interview. While closed-ended questions can sometimes be effective, open-ended questions are best for gathering information. Finally, open-ended questions give clients control over the interview compared to closed-ended questions, which give the interviewer control.

Pacing is affected by the speed of speech. The social worker needs to take time to formulate appropriate responses, respecting silence. Speaking rapidly obscures empathy and warmth. An attentive social worker must speak at a measured speed. Ineffective pacing may reduce the interview to a question and answer period instead of an in-depth interviewing session.

Quality of the Interview

The quality of an interview is affected by the lack of genuineness, empathy, warmth, and attentive listening. Other behaviors, such as premature problem solving, intimidation and judgment, and technical jargon can also negatively affect the relationship.

The social worker must be genuine and empathetic, starting with congruency between verbal and non-verbal messages. For example, "showing verbal interest" while looking at a watch suggests that interest is not genuine. Genuineness is essential. The client who believes that the worker is attending will disclose information and speak openly and honestly, especially if convinced that the social worker is genuine and empathetic. Social workers who lack warmth may also show lack of respect. Unresponsive, cold workers will be less effective.

While touch can show attending, excessive touching or touching the opposite gender inappropriately can create discomfort. Touch is a thorny issue in interviewing, especially when so many clients have a history of sexual and physical abuse. It is important to convey empathy and warmth without putting the client in a position of questioning boundaries.

Premature problem solving can also detract from the interview. The client must have the opportunity to reach his or her own decisions, based on personal competence. The most appropriate solution to the social worker may not necessarily be the best for the client. Clients must be permitted to work through issues in a way that suits them.

Clients do not come in to be judged or intimidated. The social worker must attend to what the client is sharing without imposing personal values, a task that is easier if the social worker is self-aware. Once aware of personal beliefs and biases, the social worker can refrain from reacting negatively when clients express differing views and beliefs. If clients feel intimidated or judged, they will be less likely to open up and may drop out.

In addition, social workers should "start where the client is." The client will respond better if the social worker is truly able to understand the client's problem(s). This will not happen if the social worker does not use language to fit the client, and technical jargon will be ineffective with most clients. Building upon the helping relationship is possible if both are working together. A vocabulary using the client's words, when appropriate, will be more effective and relay to the client that he or she is being heard.

Communication Barriers

Clear, direct, open, and honest communication contributes to a positive working relationship and also models communication. The road to change begins when clients make connections between emotions, thoughts, and behavior.

As a social worker, it is important to avoid judgmental communication barriers such as moralizing, judging, lecturing, praising, name-calling, and minimizing. Such behaviors make clients feel that their personal beliefs are defective or inferior and may prevent them from sharing information. Further, when the social worker espouses personal values, the client may adopt them just to please. Subsequently, the client is invalidated.

Other communication barriers that do not help include consoling, ordering, sarcasm, and random chitchat. These behaviors placate the client and reinforce inaction and indecision. Incongruencies in client behaviors are avoided, giving them no opportunity to determine their direction. As a result, the client is not expected to assume responsibility for feelings or behaviors and will not be motivated to change.

The last set of communication barriers is based on power differences; they intimidate and include threatening, probing, and analyzing. The social worker may behave in a way that is perceived as hostile, requiring clients to justify their behavior, values, and beliefs. This may result in defensiveness and a need to rationalize their maladaptive behaviors. By putting the client on the defensive, the social worker forces the client to work in opposition to the social worker. Further, clients may feel that they are expected to deal with the problem(s) alone and develop strategies to offset the intimidation. This may result in client isolation and cause the client to withdraw.

Rules to Minimize Bad Habits

Some rules that can help decrease bad habits include:

1. Always ask if there is a **better relationship building response** to give the client at this moment in time.

2. When in doubt (i.e., you do not know what good response to give a client) **BE SILENT! Being silent** can be operationalized as a **five-second count** of silence to allow time to clear thoughts and develop an appropriate response. The client will often respond after the silence and give more content to respond to on your next occasion.

3. **Silence** is often a good response when a client gives you only **one word or a short sentence response.**

4. When a client gives a long response, it is useful to **reflect back the key themes.** This makes the client feel understood.

5. It is important to reflect **all the key themes.** For example, the client says: "I am feeling very overwhelmed right now, my husband just left me, and I do not know what to do—to stay home with the kids or go find work. As well, I don't know how to tell the kids that their dad has left." In this example, there are four themes: feeling overwhelmed, husband leaving, going to work or staying at home, and telling the kids about dad leaving.

6. **Nine out of ten times in a reflection, the last thing said is what the client will talk about.** Thus, even when you think you are being non-directive, you are directing the client. In the example, if you want the client to talk about her husband leaving, you might respond with a reflection such as:

   The concerns you are having right now are making you feel overwhelmed. At the same time, you have to decide whether to stay home or go to work, and how to tell your children that their dad has left. I am sure you have a lot of issues with your husband just leaving.

   Alternatively, if you want the client to talk about her feelings, you could respond with:

   There are a number of important issues for you right now. Your husband has just left you and you are faced with the decision of staying at home or going to work, as well as figuring out how to tell your children that their dad has left. All of these issues have left you feeling very overwhelmed.

   Keep in mind that throughout the interview, you will have opportunities to discuss all the themes that appear.

7. **Show warmth!** Warmth is shown through reflective statements and through tone of voice and pacing. Warmth can also be a stand-alone response, such as: "It is really sad to hear about the loss of your pet." Warm responses convey both caring and validation of client feelings.

8. **Avoid all "why" questions.** Ask "how" or "what" questions instead.

9. To **avoid excessive questioning,** try not to ask more than two questions in a row. After two questions, respond with silence, reflection, or warmth.

10. Be aware of **excessive and unnecessary verbal utterances** and attempt to eliminate them.

11. Be aware of **non-verbal distracting behaviors,** such as excessive head nodding, and attempt to eliminate them. For example, use large upper body torso movement instead of head nodding (head bobbing) when uncomfortable. Head nodding can mean either that the interviewer is acting habitually and is not aware of the behavior, or it can mean, "Tell me more," or "I understand." A much clearer response is to say directly, "Tell me more about...." or to reflect back the key themes the client has said to show your understanding.

12. Make certain that **every** response is **intentional.** While this requires vigilance and hard work, it will also contribute to a more effective interview and allow the core conditions of empathy, warmth, and genuineness to emerge.

Conclusion

The purpose of a helping relationship is to promote growth and personal development and assist clients to develop skills that will enable them to deal with present and future problems or issues. The effectiveness of this process will depend on both the presence of relationship building skills and the elimination or minimization of "bad habits." Distracting behaviors, the pace of the interview, quality of the interview, and communication barriers presented by the social worker are all factors that affect the success of the interaction. The social worker must be aware of how his or her actions affect the client and how such behaviors influence the quality of the relationship. Minimization of bad habits and their replacement with relationship building skills enhance the client-social worker interview to allow a positive, caring, working relationship to be created.

References

Anstey, L., Bradford, D., & Yumol, L. (1998). *Dysfunctional behaviors.* Unpublished manuscript.

Collins, D. (1984). *A study of the transfer of interviewing skills from the laboratory to the field.* Unpublished doctoral dissertation, University of Toronto.

Collins, D. (1990). Identify dysfunctional counseling skill behaviors. *The Clinical Supervisor, 8* (1), 67-79.

Gorden, R. (1992). *Basic interviewing skills.* Itasca, IL: F.E. Peacock.

Lishman, J. (1994). *Communication in social work.* London: The Macmillan Press Ltd.

Termination and Your Field Placement

Joseph Walsh, Ph.D., LCSW

Termination can be defined as the process of bringing a relationship with a client to a constructive end. Most social workers are aware of the importance of the termination stage of intervention with clients. Still, the topic receives relatively little emphasis in course work and from supervisors. Termination is too often conceptualized as a process of consolidating gains already made during the intervention. Managing endings, however, requires a unique set of skills and is critical for both the student *and* the client's well being. This chapter will focus primarily on field placement terminations with clients but will also address the importance of endings with the field instructor and other agency staff.

Terminating with Clients

Whether or not a termination is managed well can make the difference between successful and unsuccessful outcomes for the client. If intervention gains are not consolidated and the worker/client relationship is not resolved, the client may not sustain his or her growth. For these reasons, the social worker has an ethical responsibility to implement a thoughtful termination plan for each client. *Closure* represents an ideal form of termination. It does not occur in every situation but characterizes endings in which the social worker and client have the opportunity to:

- bring their work to a mutually understood (but not *necessarily* satisfactory) end

181

- review the successes and failures of their work
- identify what they *each* learned from the process
- *perhaps* acknowledge mutual feelings about the relationship
- mutually experience an enhanced willingness to invest in future relationships.

The process of termination should begin during the *first meeting* with a client system. If the social worker utilizes a *time-limited* intervention strategy, it should be relatively easy to orient the client to the process from its beginning to the anticipated end. If the social worker will use *open-ended* practice models, he or she should still provide an orientation to the total process, including a review of the changes that will serve as indicators that the intervention should end. The client should be invited during the first session to give input into the process. Clients may prefer shorter or longer-term interventions, and their preferences should be respected. Finally, the student *always* knows when the field placement will end, and should make sure that clients are aware of this ending date from the beginning.

When intervention is organized with attention to termination dates or criteria, the social worker is more likely to conduct a focused intervention process and plan ahead for that ending. Listed below is a complete set of termination tasks for the social worker in a field placement to consider:

- decide when to actively implement the process
- time the announcement of one's leaving
- anticipate the client's and one's own reactions
- appropriately space the remaining sessions
- review intervention gains
- generalize intervention gains
- plan for goal maintenance
- address the client's remaining needs
- link the client with social supports (or another practitioner)
- resolve the clinical relationship
- formally evaluate the intervention (process *and* outcomes)
- set conditions and limits on future contact.

The social worker must be sensitive to the fact that the termination experience might feel very differently to the client than it does to the worker. For many social workers, termination from the field placement is one part of a celebratory process that includes college graduation, job hunting, summer break, and perhaps the beginning of a paid social work position. This might be an exciting time of transition for the social worker. For the client, the experience might only be a sad one, as a significant relationship is ending. Social workers must try to be sure that their own experiences do not impair their ability to attend to the needs of the client as that relationship ends.

Termination Rituals

Rituals provide effective ending experiences for many clients. A *ritual* is any formal activity that endows events with a sense of being special. It is most effective during times of change. Rituals symbolize continuity, stability, and the significance of personal bonds while helping people accept change. The structure of rituals provides a safe framework for social work students and their clients to express feelings about the transition. They affirm the importance of closure and imply that gains from the intervention can continue. The social worker may organize a variety of methods to celebrate a client's rite of passage. Included here are several examples of simple termination rituals.

Formal *service evaluations* provide a simple ritual with great potential to process an ending. Looking at and filling out a form objectifies the review of the intervention and relationship. It provides the client with a sense of detachment that can paradoxically facilitate expressions of feeling. It gives the client permission to respond to such questions in as much depth as he or she wishes about what it felt like to ask for help, what he or she liked most and least about the process, and how the client is planning for the future.

Expressive tasks promote communication through art forms such as painting, drawing, cutouts, music, poems, and stories. These tend to lower anxiety and stimulate emotional processing. Themes on which the social worker might focus such an ending activity include "good-bye to the old and hello to the new," best and worst memories, what the client will miss the most and least, how the transition is being experienced, and expectations about what lies ahead. Sharing picture books that contain messages about the importance of relationships can be effective with children. These activities create a parallel process, as the social worker may also experience feelings about the ending more fully.

Whether or not it is appropriate for the social worker to accept gifts from clients is a much discussed and difficult to resolve issue. Some agencies have policies on this matter, but other agencies do not, preferring that the issue be handled on a case by case basis. Some practitioners feel that clients should be permitted to express their gratitude to the social worker, and that gift giving may be the client's preferred means of doing so. Denying a client that opportunity may thus be disrespectful. Other practitioners feel that accepting gifts violates professional boundaries between the two parties, and that any expressions of gratitude can instead be made verbally. Even if the social worker does accept a gift from a client, it should be of modest material value, well within the client's means. There is a significant difference between a hand-made card and a new briefcase!

Case Illustrations

The following are examples of termination experiences of two social work students with clients in their field placements. The first was problematic and the second was more successful, but in both cases, the students faced difficult challenges in managing the ending.

What's the Point of Continuing?

I had a field placement in an adolescent services agency. Three months before the end of my placement, I was assigned to work with an 18-year-old girl named Robyn. She was having conflict with her parents, her teachers, and her friends. Robyn was not opposed to meeting with me—it may have helped that I was only five years older than she was. Robyn was quiet during our first few meetings, but her willingness to share feelings developed quickly. She had serious interpersonal problems and a fundamental inability to trust anyone. I wanted to help her explore her attitudes about relationships.

When we had met five times and had five sessions left, I reminded Robyn of my timeline, hoping that this would help us use the remaining time productively. To my surprise, she became angry. She complained that there was no point in our continuing to meet if we had to end so soon. She added that this was further proof that relationships were not worth developing because they are always transient.

I wasn't prepared for her reaction. I tried to hide my distress and shared with her my belief that she could make progress during the coming month. I assured Robyn that we would consult about a transfer to another practitioner as the end approached. She didn't accept this. Robyn came to our next four scheduled meetings but never talked openly about her presenting problems again. Our momentum was destroyed! When I tried to draw her out, she complained again that there was no point in talking because I was leaving. I became more and more frustrated. After a few weeks, I really didn't want to keep meeting with Robyn, either. I thought it might be best if I transferred her immediately. But I pressed on, trying unsuccessfully to re-engage Robyn in an intervention process. She did not show up for our final meeting. I felt that we had gotten nowhere in our last four sessions.

In retrospect, I could have used the termination issue itself as a primary theme for our discussions. I could have focused on us, and how our relationship could be worthwhile even though it had to end. I could have asked: Why did we get along well at first? How does it feel to have someone leave? Can we not keep parts of our relationships within us even as the other person moves on? What can we do together to make the best of the ending? That approach might have helped. And I should have reminded her every week about our time limits.

The Business Cards

Despite soaking up a year and a half's worth of graduate coursework, the thought of ending my intervention with Delores was baffling. My work with Delores, a 54-year-old African American woman, had been challenging because of her inability to clearly understand and express her thoughts and feelings. She often communicated with facial expressions and gestures, assuming they were sufficient for me. She also suffered from episodes in which voices in her head overwhelmed her. I was able to help her feel less anxious by teaching her deep breathing and progressive relaxation skills.

I also used solution-focused techniques to help Delores iden-
tify her strengths and act on them to accomplish her goals.

Because her thought processes were often unclear, I felt
it was appropriate to begin the ending process three months
before our last session. I began each session with a sum-
mary of our work together. She did not act surprised when I
reminded her every week of the date of our final meeting,
but I was not convinced that she understood our relationship
would in fact end. As the number of our remaining sessions
decreased, I balanced our agenda between what Delores had
achieved and what she needed to work on in the future. Ex-
actly one month from our last meeting, I started off a session
again reminding her how much time we had left. Delores
burst into tears and was unable to communicate for most of
the hour. Despite our discussing termination every week,
Delores said that she didn't truly think it would happen. I
could only remind her that it would end.

I wanted to do something special for our last meeting. I
felt it should be a celebration of Delores' hard work. We
walked to a nearby park where we sat and talked about the
progress Delores made. As a memento of our time together, I
had a stack of business cards made for Delores to carry in
her purse. On one side of the card were our names and the
dates we'd worked together. On the other side was a list of
Delores' strengths. I suggested that she read these cards
from time to time. A week later, I received a note from Delores
including one of the cards and a message that she hoped I'd
keep it in my purse.

Terminating with the Field Instructor

For many social work students, the relationship with
the field instructor becomes very close. This is the person
who has taught the student so many skills in his or her
chosen profession and who has come to know the student
so well. Social work students often develop strong feelings
about this relationship and recognize its lifelong significance.
All of the points about closure outlined earlier apply to this
relationship. How should the student address this termination? There is no particular strategy that applies to all
situations, because each relationship is different. The student should think ahead to the termination and begin to
process it with the instructor prior to the final meeting.

Near the end of my own first field placement, I wanted to talk with my field instructor about our relationship. I wanted to review our year together—to talk about how our relationship had begun awkwardly for me but evolved into one in which I felt affirmed as a young practitioner. I wanted to thank him in some special way! But he did not seem to view the significance of our ending the same way I did. Left on my own, I waited too long on that last day to talk about the year. I remember him saying to me, with only ten minutes left in our session, "What's wrong? You seem uncomfortable today." But the moment had passed. In contrast, there is a field instructor at my current agency who maintains an annual ritual of photographing her students and mounting their pictures permanently on her office wall. She then takes the students out to a big luncheon where they take the entire afternoon to review the year. This is a field instructor who is very much aware of the importance of closure!

At the very least, if the social work department requires that an evaluation form be completed at the end of the year, the mutual completion of that instrument can serve as a useful basis for a termination discussion.

Terminating with the Agency

Agency endings, while also important, are generally less complex than the other types we have considered. The emotional attachment of the student to the agency is usually less strong. Many agencies have traditions of taking students out to lunch or dinner, or having an end-of-the-year party. Even if the agency has no such celebration, the student should make a point of saying goodbye to those people who have contributed to his or her education.

Summary

The purpose of this chapter has been to describe and illustrate the importance of thoughtful termination within the field placement agency. Self-awareness and the utilization of regular supervision are the most important practices for attending to this and to other aspects of intervention. Listed below are general principles for students to use in maximizing the chances for positive endings:

- Set clear boundaries with clients about what your roles and activities *will* and *will not* include. Consistency of expectations is an excellent way to track the course of an intervention and to know when it should end.
- Be aware of your emotional and physical needs as much as possible, and be wary of obtaining too much personal gratification from your work with clients. You may, for personal reasons, decide *too soon* or *too late* to end work with a client.
- Be educated about the client's cultural and community standards of behavior, so as to understand what behaviors are reasonable to expect when formulating ending activities.
- Use *peer* consultation routinely—many practitioners learn as much from their colleagues as from formally designated supervisors.
- Refer to the *NASW Code of Ethics*, when applicable, for guidance in decision-making about termination.

Recommended Readings

Brill, M. & Nahamani, N. (1993). Clients' responses to separation from social work trainees. *Journal of Teaching in Social Work, 7* (2), 97-111.

Fortune, A. E. (1994). Termination in direct practice. In R. L. Edwards (Ed.), *Encyclopedia of Social Work* (pp. 2398-2404). Silver Spring, MD: National Association of Social Workers.

McRoy, R. G., Freeman, E. M., & Logan, S. (1986). Strategies for teaching students about termination. *The Clinical Supervisor, 4* (4), 45-56.

Pearson, Q. M. (1998). Terminating before counseling has ended: Counseling implications and strategies for counselor relocation. *Journal of Mental Health Counseling, 20* (1), 55-63.

Resnick, C., & Dziegielewski, S. F. (1996). The relationship between therapeutic termination and job satisfaction among medical social workers. *Social Work in Health Care, 23* (3), 17-33.

22

Facing Ethical Dilemmas in the Field

by Denise Anderson, Ph.D., MSW

Social work students enter the field with the knowledge, values, and skills acquired during the previous years of their formal social work education. They can often recite the theories that will guide their practice, the many skills of all phases of social work practice, and many can even recite parts of the NASW *Code of Ethics*. Many feel very prepared for entering into their field practicum experiences as generalist social work students. Despite all of the case studies, examples, and discussions about ethical dilemmas, the transition from classroom to field can be very rocky when faced with dilemmas that transcend students' preparation.

Undergraduate students from a variety of placement settings, including an alternative school setting, long term care facility, domestic violence program, mental health facility, and children and youth setting, shared with me their ethical dilemmas and guidelines for dealing with dilemmas during their senior field practicum experiences.

Confidentiality

We talk of protecting confidentiality of consumers of services, yet many of our agencies informally share information with others within and outside of the agency. Rationales for sharing this information can include: "It is really for the consumer" or "They will never know anyway." The *Code of Ethics* clearly addresses how social workers are to handle confidentiality, but what happens when agency workers are not social work-educated workers? For field students, confronting or questioning agency employees is difficult, especially early in the semester before relationships are established.

One student found herself in a situation in which a worker talked openly to other workers about client information that did not pertain to their caseloads, nor was it used to gain consultation about the case. As the student observed the interaction, her concern grew. Should she report this to her supervisor, talk to her professor, confront the workers, or keep it to herself? She asked herself, *am I making a big deal out of this, or is this an important enough issue to bring to others' attention?*

When this was discussed in the next field seminar session, many students reported similar situations that had occurred in their particular settings, both with social work and non-social work educated persons. Upon discussing this issue, some were led to believe by their agencies that "it is not a big deal" and "it happens in the field—all information is kept within the agency."

In another example, a high school student shared information with a social work student who was working as an educator in a domestic violence situation. One of the student's assignments was to run a teen pregnancy group in a high school. "One girl in particular, who is 15 years old, is having the child of a 25-year-old man," the high schooler confided to the social work student. After this student worker asked the guidance counselor about this issue, she was told, "It happens all the time."

"I guess my main concern is how to press (this issue), without getting or being in the business of the family. Being a professional, I know that I have the right (and responsibility) to uphold the law, but at the same time, I am a guest in the host setting of a school."

The student was not sure of her role. Should she "go above the head" of the school guidance counselor, who dismissed the issue, to report the crime of the man's sexual involvement with a minor?

Client Right to Self Determination

Another common ethical dilemma for students in the field is assuring clients' right to self-determination. There are times when what may seem best for the client is not what they, or, in health care situations, their power of attorney deem best.

One such example involved an elderly female resident of a nursing home. She had open wounds related to diabetes, and an infection resulted from the wounds. Since antibiotics were not effective, the doctor recommended amputation, which he felt would prolong her life. The family, who was serving as her power of attorney, decided on comfort measures only. This reflected what she had indicated to them prior to her inability to make her own decisions. The social work student struggled with allowing her to remain in some pain and not taking action, when the doctor felt confident her life could be extended.

While this didn't require extensive decision making, since the *Code of Ethics* is clear about client right to self determination, the worker did struggle with whether or not the family had the resident's best interest in mind. Although this had been discussed in class with case studies, dealing with this in "real life" is significantly different. "It is a difficult thing to do, however, because it means watching the woman die a slow but certain death," the student said.

Another example of dealing with client rights occurred in a mental health facility. The student worker observed a client who was not cooperating with the program, but did not present a harm to self or others. The staff decided that because he was not following the rules, he needed a "break" from the program. He was told that he would be allowed to return after a few weeks' break, if he agreed to follow the program rules. In this situation, the student felt that the client needed services for his apparent symptoms of psychosis, which seemed to be causing his behavior difficulties.

Since the student worker was fairly new to the situation, as well as the field in general, she did not feel qualified to question the decision-makers in the agency.

Handling Ethical Dilemmas in the Field

How should students handle ethical dilemmas in the field? Students who dealt with ethical issues during their field practica shared some ideas with me and each other. Their collective answers include:

1. *Discuss the issue or concerns with your field instructor.*
    The purpose of the field instructor is to serve as an edu-
    cator in the field setting. One of the reasons the Council
    on Social Work Education requires the instructor to have
    a BSW or MSW is to help the student integrate the knowl-
    edge, values, and skills learned during the educational
    tenure. If there is a concern about the instructor, then
    the student needs to discuss the issue with the faculty
    liaison or other social work faculty.

2. *Research and know the NASW Code of Ethics.* Several
    textbooks have components of the *Code*, it is online, and
    it is available by writing or calling NASW. In other words,
    there is no reason for social work students to not be
    aware of the *Code*. While the *Code* does not provide pre-
    scriptive measures for dealing with ethical dilemmas, it
    provides clear guidelines by which to practice.

3. *Discuss the issue with your faculty liaison and peers.*
    Social work programs offer a seminar component in con-
    junction with the field experience. Usually, this is an
    opportunity for additional knowledge dissemination, as
    well as peer and faculty consultation. Discussing the is-
    sues with peers allows for others to gain from one expe-
    rience, as well as feedback from several sources. The
    faculty liaison's role includes serving as educator, liai-
    son, and mediator in field issues and learning.

4. *Examine what seems to be the best interest of the client.*
    From all of the information that has been gathered about
    the client system, including his/her/their perspective,
    start where they are at that point in time. Sometimes
    this means gathering additional information before act-
    ing on a situation.

5. *Recognize other professions' Codes of Ethics.* Doctors,
    nurses, lawyers, teachers, and other professionals do not
    have the same guiding code as social workers. Under-
    stand the differences, so as not to assume someone in
    authority has the "right" answer. Also important in rec-
    ognizing differences is to learn to respect the
    uniquenesses of other practice professions. While other
    professions' codes may differ and sometimes conflict, it

is important to be aware of and respect these differences and driving forces for practice.

6. *Educate yourself on the laws and rules guiding the particular field of practice/setting of field placement.* Each field has its own set of laws or practice rules, such as child welfare laws of reporting child abuse, mental health laws for voluntary and involuntary commitments to treatment, and so forth. While it is best to have an awareness and understanding of all social work-related laws, it is critical to understand those in each particular field.

The bottom line is that each setting is different and no matter how prepared each student might be from courses, case studies, and other readings, situations can present a struggle. It is important to know how and where to search for answers.

23

Ethics:
Issues for Interns

by Katherine M. Dunlap, Ph.D., ACSW,
and Kimberly Strom-Gottfried, Ph.D., MSW, LISW

Authors' Note: The authors wish to thank the students who submitted questions and Natalie Whisenant, MSW, for identifying the connection between Erikson and ethics.

While it is true, then, that as scientists we must study ethics objectively, we are, as professional individuals, committed to a unification of personality, training, and conviction which alone will help us do our work adequately.

Erik Erikson, 1964

In 1960, the NASW *Code of Ethics* consisted of only 14 statements. The current code, ratified in 1996, contains 155 specific ethical standards. According to Reamer (1998), these reflect increased knowledge in the profession. They are "designed to guide social workers' conduct, reduce malpractice and liability risks, and provide a basis for adjudication of ethics complaints field against NASW members" (p. 495).

The current *Code* addresses three types of issues: 1) "mistakes" by well-meaning workers, 2) difficult ethical decisions, and 3) ethical misconduct (Reamer, 1998). This chapter will look at two questions from students and suggest ways to prevent common "mistakes"—actions of commission or omission that might have ethical implications.

What Should I Call Myself?

I am a mature worker with 15 years of experience in the same agency. Last year, I decided to pursue a social work degree through a part-time program. My professor says that my nametag should indicate my student status. I'm afraid this will alienate my clients. I also worry that co-workers will think I am less capable.

This is a complicated query. Student/employees often feel vulnerable when they begin field practice in an agency setting. Your intent is to provide excellent care and service, as you have always done. At the same time, you know that mistakes are inevitable when you are learning new skills. How can you grow and stretch while protecting your clients from unintentional blunders? This is a delicate balance. Fortunately, the *Code* provides direction through several different standards.

Learning is a Team Affair

Student/employees are responsible for protecting clients. How can you accomplish this? Section 3.02 of the NASW *Code of Ethics* addresses ethical responsibilities regarding education and training in practice settings.

Social workers who function as educators or field instructors for students should take reasonable steps to ensure that clients are routinely informed when services are being provided by students. (3.02 c)

This is the standard that requires you to identify your student status on your nametag. Embedded in this standard are guidelines that protect you, your clients, and your agency while you are learning.

This standard points to the teaching triad of you, your field instructor (who is probably employed at the agency where you are placed), and your faculty liaison. You have probably noticed that the onus or responsibility for fulfilling these standards is placed on the educator and field instructor. This is because they have already attained the professional degree, and they can be held accountable for their actions. As a student, you are not expected to have all of the answers yet.

The three of you should function as a team to help you get those answers. Learning can be intense and trying, as well as exhilarating. It is as important to be intentional about developing your learning team as it is to be intentional about establishing a treatment team or any other work group.

At the beginning of the semester, take time to talk about your learning styles. Explore the ways that you prefer to receive feedback and establish communication channels. Explain the grading standards of your school, and review evaluation procedures. Your goal is to establish a close relationship in which you can share your trials and your tribulations, your joys and your accomplishments.

This close relationship facilitates meaningful, purposeful supervision that enhances your professional self and your efforts on behalf of your clients. Appropriate supervision also protects the agency from errors of judgment (Houston-Vega, Nuehring, & Daguio, 1997; NASW, 1994). Hopefully, your colleagues will see the positive changes you are making and commend you for accepting the powerful challenge of returning to school for your degree.

Learning is a Process

Social workers should provide services and represent themselves as competent only within the boundaries of their education, training, license, certification, consultation received, supervised experience, or other relevant professional experience. (1.04a)

Social workers should provide services in substantive areas or use intervention techniques or approaches that are new to them only after engaging in appropriate study, training, consultation, and supervision from people who are competent in those interventions or techniques. (1.04b)

These standards and the ones that came before acknowledge that learning is a process, which proceeds through reasonable steps. In field, these steps are enumerated and elaborated in the Learning Plan, sometimes called a Learning Agreement or Learning Contract.

Your learning team will help you develop a plan that identifies reasonable, realistic goals that build on your strengths as a seasoned worker. The learning plan should push you to develop new skills and try new strategies, but it should set guidelines for the way you go about garnering new skills. The guidelines specify the tasks that will enable you to meet your goals.

For example, imagine that your goal is to master play therapy with children. If you have never attempted play therapy, it would be inappropriate for you to begin by sitting on the floor with a child and a box of toys. Rather, you would expect to learn the theories and principles of play therapy from your professors, your field instructor, and other experts in your region.

After you have mastered the basics, you might observe others conducting play therapy sessions. You would discuss your impressions with the therapists, and you might even write a paper incorporating what you have learned with what you have observed.

Next, you might co-lead a play therapy session with your field instructor. Again, this experience would be followed by discussion and analysis. Finally, when you have a good grasp of the techniques, you might conduct a session while your field instructor observes you. After several sessions, you could present a case summary highlighting the role of play therapy for your treatment team.

This vignette highlights the importance of process in social work education. Like our clients, we learn in small steps. One way to protect others is to be sure that no step in the process is too big. This is not the time to leap! When you leap, you risk a fall that could hurt yourself and others.

Through the process of field education, the learning team works together to oversee opportunities for you to grow and develop while protecting clients and the agency from errors that could harm them.

On the other hand, if the tasks available in the placement merely repeat your experience as an employee, this probably is not an appropriate educational experience. After all, the goal of education is to stretch and grow.

What Can I Share?

I have received several assignments that require me to talk about my cases at school. I am placed in a public agency, and some of our clients have been in the news recently. Their situations are very interesting and complex. I would like to ask my professors' opinions about treatment and policy issues, but I don't want to violate confidentiality. What can I share in class?

Several ethical standards apply to this situation. The first involves a principle called "the need to know."

The "Need to Know"

Social workers should respect clients' right to privacy. Social workers should not solicit private information from clients unless it is essential to providing services or conducting social work evaluation or research. Once private information is shared, standards of confidentiality apply. (1.07a)

In other words, you should obtain only the data you need to make sound clinical decisions. You should not ask questions out of curiosity, and you should not pry into areas unrelated to the presenting problem or treatment plan. If you adhere to the "need to know" principle, you will not have inappropriate material to share with others.

The "need to know" principle guides data collection, but it does not answer your question directly. Under what conditions can you share pertinent case information?

Check the Agency Agreement

Before you were placed in a field assignment, the agency and the school established a contract that specified the conditions of your placement. Often, these agreements address patient confidentiality. Before sharing any information, review the agency placement agreement on file at the school.

Disguise Information

You may share information that is totally disguised, but disguising involves changing more than names and demographics. You must camouflage all identifying information to be certain that others cannot guess or surmise the identity of a client. If this is impossible, as it often is in high profile cases, you should refrain from using a case in class, no matter how interesting it may be.

Share with Consent

Social workers should not disclose identifying information when discussing clients for teaching or training purposes unless the client has consented to disclosure of confidential information. (1.07q)

Generally, when there is no threat of danger to self or others, material shared by clients remains their property. Although you heard this information, it is not your property or even the property of your supervisor or your agency. Professionals use information in order to serve the client. The client must give informed consent before information can be shared with others (Cournoyer, 1996).

Agencies that regularly train interns often have official Informed Consent Statements, which include permission to train interns, to present scientific findings in which data are anonymous, and to consult with experts outside the agency.

It is important to understand that anonymous is not the same as confidential. According to Rubin and Babbie (1993), a client is anonymous only when the practitioner cannot link a particular response with a particular person. This means that a face-to-face interview can never be anonymous, since the practitioner collects information from an identifiable source (p. 60).

Confidentiality is different. Confidentiality means that you know what an individual has said and you promise not to reveal this information to anyone without informed consent or the right to know, in cases of potential harm (Dickson, 1998).

Houston-Vega, Nuehring, and Daguio present a sample form that allows clients to check those items that are acceptable to them (1997, C-25). This form states that any further disclosure requires additional discussion and another consent form. It also says that material should only be shared with other professionals or with other trainees who are also ethically obligated to protect confidentiality.

Even with appropriate consent to share information, you should use pseudonyms and disguise identifying information. You should also begin your presentations by reminding the audience of their personal responsibility to protect the client's privacy. These precautions ensure beneficence, respect, and justice, three ethical principles that should underlie all research activities, including training (Anastas & MacDonald, 1994).

Conclusion

Erikson, in concluding his discussion of ethics and the Golden Rule, recounted the following anecdote, which serves as a good model for all social workers:

> *Rabbi Hillel once was asked by an unbeliever to tell the whole of the Torah while he stood on one foot. I do not know whether he meant to answer the request or to remark on its condition when he said: "What is hateful to yourself, do not to your fellow man. That is the whole of the Torah and the rest is but commentary." At any rate, he did not add: "Act accordingly." He said: "Go, and learn it."*

References

Anastas, J. W., & MacDonald, M. L. *Research design for social work and the human services.* New York: Lexington.

Cournoyer, B. (1996). *The social work skills workbook* (2nd Ed.). Pacific Grove, CA: Brooks/Cole.

Dickson, D. T. (1998). *Confidentiality and privacy in social work: A guide to the law for practitioners and students.* New York: Free Press.

Erikson, E. H. (1964). *Insight and responsibility: Lectures on the ethical implications of psychoanalytic insight.* New York: W. W. Norton.

Houston-Vega, M. K., Nuehring, E. M., & Daguio, E.R. (1997). *Prudent practice: A guide for managing malpractice risk.* Washington, D.C.: NASW Press.

National Association of Social Workers. (1960). *NASW Code of Ethics.* New York: Author.

National Association of Social Workers. (1996). *NASW Code of Ethics*. Washington, D.C.: Author.

National Association of Social Workers, National Council on the Practice of Clinical Social Work. (1994). *Guidelines for clinical social work supervision.* Washington, D.C.: Author.

Reamer, F. G. (1998). The evolution of social work ethics. *Social Work, 43* (6), 488-500.

Rubin, A., & Babbie, E. (1993). *Research methods for social work* (2nd Ed.). Pacific Grove, CA: Brooks/Cole.

Promoting Social Justice Within the Practicum

by Julie Birkenmaier, MSW, LCSW

Anthony, in his second semester at a youth emergency shelter, has conducted assessments, counseled clients, and collected data for an agency evaluation research project. During his site visit, his faculty liaison inquired about his plans to promote social justice during his practicum. He has not observed any staff engaging in any activities that address social justice. Although he learned about the importance of social justice to the social work profession, he feels lost. What should he tell his faculty liaison? How can he promote social justice in his direct practice practicum?

Social Justice and the Social Work Profession

In addition to work on behalf of individuals, historical precedence exists for social workers' promotion of social justice. Dating back to the efforts of such social workers as Jane Addams, social workers have struggled for peace and social justice since the 19th century (Van Soest, 1995). Social workers have recently promoted social justice for such oppressed populations as gays and lesbians, people of color, and other vulnerable groups (Van Soest, 1995). The *Code of Ethics* (NASW, 1996) mandates a commitment to social justice as a core value of the profession through social welfare, public participation, and social and political action (Section 6.01, 6.02 and 6.04). Social workers are called to "...advocate for living conditions conducive to the fulfillment of basic human needs and...promote social, economic, political and cultural values and institutions that are compatible with the realization of social justice" (NASW, 1996). The *Code* mandates that "social workers should engage in social and political action that seeks to ensure that all people have equal access to the resources, employment, services and opportunities they require to meet their basic human needs and to develop fully" (NASW, 1996). Social workers are also required to prevent and eliminate the domination, exploitation of and discrimination against any person, group, or class (NASW, 1996).

Social work students are also expected to learn about and promote social and economic justice. This mandate is embodied in the standards for accredited BSW and MSW social work programs from the Council on Social Work Education (Council on Social Work Education, 1994). The accreditation standards mandate programs to "...provide students with the skills to promote social change and to implement a wide range of interventions that advance the achievement of individual and collective social and economic justice" (Council on Social Work Education, 1994).

Social Justice Defined

What is and how does one promote social justice? Even with a strong mandate, social justice remains undefined in the *Code of Ethics* (NASW, 1996). In general, the concept of social justice addresses fairness, equity, and equality (Flynn, 1995). Although a universal definition of social justice has yet to be developed, Van Soest (1995) has identified three contemporary views: 1) legal justice (i.e., an individual's obligations to society), 2) commutative justice (i.e., obligations between individuals), and 3) distributive justice (i.e., society's debts to an individual). Social workers have traditionally focused on distributive justice as they strive to prevent injustices and oppression by seeking responsiveness to needs at the structural or institutional level. Social workers have worked to eliminate oppression (between individuals, social groups, classes, and societies based on race, ethnicity, abilities, sexual orientation, and other characteristics) and injustices, such as "coercively established and maintained inequalities, discrimination and dehumanizing conditions of living" (Gil, 1998, p. 10). Contemporary advocacy efforts focus on inadequate health care for the poor, the dearth of decent, affordable housing, inadequate public education, unemployment, lack of livable wage employment, regressive taxation, nutritional justice, and domestic violence. Social action activities include lobbying (through face-to-face contact, letter writing, e-mail, and telephone contact), demonstrations, testifying before committees, media work (press conferences, letters to the editor, and op-ed pieces), and civil disobedience actions.

Social Justice Promotion

Despite the mandate and calls for action, most contemporary social workers report that they do not engage in efforts to address social injustices (Borenzweig, 1981; Brill, 1990). While most social workers limit their professional activities to those of helping people live with and adjust to conditions of injustice and oppression by alleviating symptoms, a minority of social workers address the roots of injustice and oppression and help people organize for empowerment (Gil, 1998). Those social workers who incorporate social justice activities into their professional work choose to do so for a wide variety of causes and from a spectrum of settings. Social workers' primary practice modalities—direct/clinical or indirect—are important factors in their involvement in social justice activities.

Direct Practice

As 70% of social workers report direct practice as their primary function (Gibelman & Schervish, 1997), integrating social justice promotion with direct practice is a focus of continuing professional discussion. Activities to promote social justice within direct practice include:

- collecting and submitting clients' life stories, including perspectives about current problems and their vision of justice related to a specific topic to decision-makers (e.g., agency administrators or legislators) (Freeman, 1997),
- empowering clients to participate in social action activities,
- engaging in social action activities as a private citizen or as an agency or coalition representative, and
- promoting the organization of mutual aid groups to take collective action on an issue (Swenson, 1998).

Indirect Practice

Indirect practice is a primary focus for a smaller number of social workers (17%). The majority of those engaged in macro practice as a primary function report management as their primary function (Gibelman & Schervish, 1997). Many options exist for the pursuit of social justice within an *administrative* level of an agency, to include (Flynn, 1995):

* creating and/or utilizing a client and/or staff grievance procedure,
* advocating for funding of a new initiative during the annual budget process, and
* providing substantive input into administrative decision-making processes on a social justice issue.

Advocates can use agency charters, articles of incorporation, licensing and/or accreditation standards, formal and/or informal agency policies and pressure from outside influences, such as funding entities and professional associations, as sources of legitimacy for advocacy at an agency level on a particular issue (Flynn, 1995).

Social workers involved in *policy practice* engage in social policy analysis, legislative advocacy, reform through litigation, and social action (Figueira-McDonald, 1993) and address social injustices through direct involvement in the policy-making process. *Researchers* can address social injustices through empowerment of research subjects (Sarri & Sarri, 1992) and use findings for advocacy efforts against social injustices. *Community practitioners* empower neighborhood residents and communities to address injustices and/or oppression.

Students and Social Justice

As you discuss your practicum requirements and learning activities with your field instructor, consider possibilities for promoting social justice during your practicum.

For practica focused primarily on direct practice, social justice activities can begin with client experiences. Integral to any social work intervention is consideration of the societal oppression and injustices that have an impact on clients. Possible effects of such structural factors as unemployment, discrimination, poverty, malnutrition, and other issues that have shaped clients' lives and needs must be addressed. Seek to raise clients' consciousness regarding the impact of these conditions of social injustices (through individual, family, and/or group work) and encourage participation in social action activities (Gil, 1998).

Examine possibilities for your direct involvement in social action that promotes social change during your practicum. Areas to explore include committees, groups or coalitions of which your agency or field instructor is a professional member; or social action activities in which the agency or the field instructor participates (independent of an organizational affiliation).

If the agency or field instructor cannot identify an opportunity for social action, consider social action activities of affiliated agencies in which you could participate, or advocacy efforts of which you are aware that you would like to include in your practicum activities.

After a social justice issue and a forum for social action have been identified, discussion then can center on your role. The extent of your involvement in an activity depends on your practicum requirements, the extent to which opportunities are available during your practicum, and your other responsibilities. The possibilities for your role are limitless. Some examples include:

- attend domestic violence coalition meetings and participate in a lobby day
- assist an affiliated welfare rights organization to organize and prepare recipients of public assistance to demonstrate against new regulations at a public assistance office
- gather data on the negative impact of Medicaid managed care for clients and testify before a state legislative commission
- draft a letter to a county commissioner or other elected official (to be approved by the agency director) regarding the needs of the chronically mentally ill
- help organize a press conference (e.g., send out press releases, contact potential speakers, and compile press packets) regarding a new study of the state's homeless population.

Seizing Opportunities: Challenges and Strategies

While promoting social justice is an important learning experience, challenges may arise. These may include:

1. *Advocate Credibility.* Effective advocacy efforts depend upon the advocate's credibility with the decision-making person or entity. Credibility is gained through a series of interactions over time with the target group. As a student, your credibility as an advocate may be limited (Flynn, 1995). Joining with the efforts of other professionals or organizations/coalitions involved in an effort can dramatically increase your credibility and effectiveness. If a two-semester placement is an option, consider using this time to build your credibility through experience and exposure to decision-makers.

2. *Available Modeling and Resources.* If your field instructor may not engage in activities that promote social justice, you can cultivate relationships with other professionals for exposure to and resources for advocacy efforts.

3. *Sanction.* If your practicum site does not engage in or encourage advocacy activities, consider negotiating with your field instructor and faculty liaison to participate in activities that relate to social justice as a private individual (rather than as an agency representative).

4. *Time Constraints.* Your other practicum responsibilities may be so consuming that to add activities to promote social justice would be difficult. Negotiation and planning are key to managing one's time. When possible, include at least one social justice activity into the initial agreed-upon activities or negotiate the termination/transfer of cases/activities so that you may include social justice activities.

5. *Expectation of "Success."* A successful social justice advocate must often continue tireless efforts over a long period of time (Flynn, 1995). Your role as a practicum

student is, by definition, time limited. Your opportunities to have an impact on a social justice issue are constrained by a brief time frame or the scale of the effort. Defining "process" goals (i.e., skills to be utilized during the advocacy effort) and clarifying your role(s) and responsibilities as an advocate are essential to your success and satisfaction.

6. *Fear.* Many helping professionals find advocacy intimidating and challenging and cite fear as an obstacle to overcoming complacency. If your fear inhibits your motivation to promote social justice, consider your prior experiences with new activities. As you begin to engage in activities to promote social justice, allow yourself the freedom to make some mistakes and remember that you are there to learn (that IS what practicum is all about!).

Conclusion

After discussion with his field instructor and faculty liaison, Anthony began to document the basic needs issues that arose for his clients. At the next site visit, Alex reported that the lack of decent, affordable housing was common among many of his clients seeking reunification with their teenage children. To engage in an advocacy effort to address this issue, Alex attended meetings of an affordable housing advocacy group and accompanied advocates on a visit to a city councilperson to discuss housing issues.

The foundation for a commitment to advance social justice is the ability to discern structural and societal issues as central to the clients' problems. While many client issues involve areas for which clients can make individual adjustments, many individual problems have roots in the structures of our society and culture. This commitment is fulfilled when action is taken to attempt to remedy environmental injustices and oppression.

Your practicum experience significantly influences your career. Addressing social injustices during this learning experience can both enhance your commitment to social justice and aid in efforts to increase your clients' quality of life. Even when not incorporated into your primary professional role, you are called to promote social change. Seek opportunities to address social injustices during your practicum. These experiences will be beneficial for you and your future clients and strengthen your ties to the profession's *Code of Ethics* (1996).

References

Brill, C. K. (1990). *The impact on social work practice of the social injustice content in the NASW Code of Ethics.* Doctoral dissertation, Brandeis University.

Borenzweig, H. (1981). Agency vs. private practice: Similarities and differences. *Social Work, 26* (3), 239-33.

Council on Social Work Education. (1994). *Handbook of accreditation standards and procedures.* Alexandria, VA: Author.

Figueira-McDonald, J. (1993). Policy practice: The neglected side of social work intervention. *Social Work, 38* (2), 179-88.

Flynn, J, P. (1995). Social justice in social agencies. In *Encyclopedia of Social Work* (19th edition). Washington, D.C.: NASW Press.

Freeman, E. M. (1997). Alternative stories and narratives for transforming schools, families, communities and policymakers. *Social Work in Education, 19* (2), 67-71.

Gibelman, M., & Schervish, P. H. (1997). *Who we are: A second look.* Washington, D.C.: NASW Press.

Gil, D. G. (1998). *Confronting injustice and oppression: Concepts and strategies for social workers.* New York: Columbia University Press.

National Association of Social Workers (1996). *Code of ethics.* Washington, D.C.: NASW Press.

Sarri, R., & Sarri, C. (1992). Participatory action research in two communities in Bolivia and the United States. *International Social Work, 35* (2), 267-80.

Swenson, C. R. (1998). Clinical social work's contribution to a social justice perspective. *Social Work, 43* (6), 527-537.

Van Soest, D. (1995). Peace and social justice. In *Encyclopedia of Social Work* (19th edition). Washington, D.C.: NASW Press.

The author wishes to thank Marla Berg-Weger, PhD, Assistant Professor and Director of Practicum at Saint Louis University School of Social Service, for her invaluable assistance with this article.

25

Counting Blessings

by Angela Allen, BSW

Editor's Note: The following was written by Angela Allen for her internship seminar four weeks prior to her completion of the BSW program at Appalachian State University in Boone, NC. This represents one student's list of "blessings." Can you count your own?

I just read an article entitled, "Fifty Proven Stress Reducers." Number 32 says, "For every one thing that goes wrong, there are 50 to 100 blessings. Count them."

Something went wrong today. Can I count 50 blessings that are related to my internship? I can try.

1. I could be in a factory sewing Hardee's uniforms.

2. I could be at Hardee's.

3. Graduation is May 10!

4. I'm still a student, and stupid mistakes are to be expected on rare occasions.

5. Every day, I see someone who makes me feel thankful for my eyes, ears, brains, clothes, parents, car (!), and so on....

6. It's a good feeling to know you've helped someone who really needs it.

7. Compared to most peoples' standards, my life is successful.

8. My daughter has a mother who will graduate from college on May 10.

9. Sara (supervisor) is really understanding and patient.

10. Dr. G. is really understanding and patient.

11. I am learning to be really understanding and patient.

12. It's almost over.

13. There are still three social work jobs here.*

14. Two months from now, I will buy my groceries with cash instead of food stamps for the first time in four years.

15. I am bound to get gifts of money when I graduate.

16. One of my clients almost cried when I told her I was leaving in May.

17. One man is not going to die because he can't get his heart medicine.

18. The Girl Scouts are going to the nursing home to visit.

19. My office window has a beautiful view of mountains and (today) a cloudless, Tarheel blue sky.

20. I am not a lawyer!

21. I will have a retirement account started before I am thirty.

22. It's a good feeling to know that a client trusts your judgment and motives.

23. I have unlimited opportunities to face reality.

24. I have unlimited opportunities to face myself.

25. My daughter will grow up with a sympathetic, caring perspective on life. Already, she takes care of me at times. Twice in the last month I have said, "Natalie, we aren't going to be poor much longer." Both times, her reply was, "We're not poor! If we were poor, we wouldn't have a house, or a car, or a TV, or food, or clothes, or beds, or a toilet,

or a Nintendo, or books." I can't be too bad if I'm her mother.

26. I get to take an hour out of my day to eat lunch and run errands. I've never had a job that gave me a whole hour before.

27. I get to be around other people who care about others as much as I do.

28. I receive respect from these same people.

29. I truly believe I can make a difference.

30. I can shut the office door and cry if I want to.

31. I love my clients.

32. Some of my clients love me back.

33. All of my clients make me laugh, in a good way.

34. One of my clients calls me "Angel."

35. One of my clients insists on actively trying to find me a husband.

36. One of my clients went from taking 13 different medicines to taking only 5.

37. Mistakes are excellent learning tools.

38. I don't *have* to be a social worker—I *want* to be.

39. I'm so tired when I get home that I haven't had trouble sleeping in a long time.

40. I don't have to drive to Boone and back every day.

41. I am making useful contacts.

42. I am learning to utilize resources.

43. I am learning excellent telephone communication skills.

44. I have a big desk now.

45. Somebody new started working here who has excellent friendship potential.

46. Some days are diamonds.

47. I get to leave the office a lot.

48. I get to come back when I do leave.

49. It's nice to get to practice before you actually get paid.

50. For every one thing that goes wrong, there are 50 or 100 blessings!

I did it! And it really does work! I was shaking when I started, but I feel better now.

*Six months later, one of these jobs is mine!

PART VI

MOVING ON

PART VI: MOVING ON

You will take what you have learned in your field placement with you throughout your career as a professional social worker. Some students are eventually hired by their field placement agencies. Others move on to paid positions in agencies similar to their field placements, while still others transfer the skills they have learned to completely different settings.

Whatever your career path, your field placement has provided you with a foundation upon which you can build and grow in the days and years ahead. You will likely look back on your field placement with the knowing smile of a survivor.

26

The Portfolio Approach for Generalist Social Work Students

by Sarah Simon, MSW, and Mona C. S. Schatz, DSW

As you near the end of your formal studies, there are decisions ahead and transitions occurring. What will you, the new social worker, do after graduation? Where will you live? With what agency or population(s) will you want to work? You have to prepare yourself for the "real world."

During this time of transition, graduating social work students are finding new ways to prepare themselves. At Colorado State University (CSU), senior social work students, in their field placement experience, address many of these issues through the development of a professional portfolio notebook, developed in conjunction with a weekly seminar where students discuss their development as a beginning social worker. Students build a portfolio notebook and use this approach as a bridge in their professional development. We asked students and field supervisors/instructors to evaluate this new learning strategy.

The Portfolio Approach: Primary Purpose

Demonstrating one's competence in practice is a vital part of good social work. The Council on Social Work Education requires all graduating social workers, undergraduate and graduate, to be able to assess and evaluate their practice. Finding tools that promote this requirement and that complement the teaching milieu and the agency practice arena is difficult. Yet, the concept of a self-reflective learning assignment for the newly emerging social worker seems a good fit for students in the conjunctive experience of class and field learning.

A *portfolio* is a notebook used to accumulate selected materials from the social work field placement experience. Primarily, the portfolio materials illustrate the student's professional skill development in the agency, along with personal achievements. Throughout the semester in placement, students find examples of different social work activities— such as assessment, intervention planning, contracting, resource development, and evaluating—and they put examples of the work into their portfolio notebooks.

Using portfolios to display one's professional work is not new. Artists, educators, and even primary and secondary students, in open-learning type environments, have used this approach. Edgerton (1991) and Herr (1992) both described the use of teaching portfolios by educators. Schon (1983) and others addressed the importance of reflection to professional development. No previously published articles exist that describe the application of portfolios by students or faculty in social work.

How Students Build a Portfolio

A portfolio is developed by (1) collecting information from the field placement agency, (2) gathering examples of social work practice done by the student, and (3) identifying different social work concepts through class-focused assignments. The chart on the next two pages provides an overview of what students incorporate into their portfolios. As shown, students include their intended learning objectives for the field experience, along with their periodic evaluations. Items such as the agency's description, the resources connected to the agency, and the agency's approach give students the opportunity to identify and describe their practice setting. Enclosing samples of agency tasks (names and identifying information blocked out) performed by beginning social workers—such as assessments, client intervention summaries, case notes, and administrative-type materials—promote the uniqueness of each student's experience in the field placement.

A portfolio becomes as extensive and elaborate as the student wants. Generally, students spend about an hour a

	SUMMARY OF STUDENTS' (N=19) RATINGS OF IMPORTANCE OF INCLUDING PORTFOLIO ITEMS	
	Required or Suggested Portfolio Item	Students' Average Rating on 5-Point Scale
1.	Learning objectives for field placement	4.42
2.	Mid-term and final evaluation reports	4.05
3.	Sample assessment (preferably multi-level)	3.94
4.	Description of how agency works with people of diverse backgrounds and cultures	3.79
5.	Summary of any professional and agency training programs student attended	3.47
6.	Notes from meetings student had specific responsibility for, or was an active member	3.42
7.	Student's own emerging social work practice model	4.11
8.	Description of a termination process	3.58
9.	A sample plan addressing an agency issue, policy concern or controversy, etc.	3.68
10.	Current résumé	4.11
11.	Sample client contract or intervention plan	3.68
12.	Samples of written materials developed by student	3.58
13.	Samples of agency materials that describe the agency's work done by student	3.94
14.	Summary of agency's practice approach, how agency does/does not use generalist approach	3.79

(continued on next page)

week focused on the portfolio project. In this hour, students may examine what they want to consider including in their notebooks. They may work on gathering materials from the agency, or work on a class assignment related to their learning.

How Students Feel About the Portfolio

Because of the newness of the portfolio approach, we asked students to provide feedback at mid-semester, and

	Required or Suggested Portfolio Item	Students' Average Rating on 5-Point Scale
	SUMMARY OF STUDENTS' (N=19) RATINGS OF IMPORTANCE OF INCLUDING PORTFOLIO ITEMS	
15.	Overview of organization, e.g. structure	3.68
16.	Sample week's schedule in the agency	2.47
17.	A practice research or evaluation project	3.79
18.	Description of typical ethical issue	3.89
19.	A list or map of how the agency works with and connects with services in community	3.68
20.	Examples of agency's generalist orientation	3.61
21.	Any media coverage while in the agency	2.72

again at the end of the semester when the portfolio was completed.

At the mid-point, students were asked to comment on what they believed to be the benefits and successes of the portfolio. In response, eighty percent (80%) of the students felt that the portfolio would be helpful to them when completed. The general consensus of these students was that they would be able to use the portfolio both for their current learning experience and for future employment interviews and résumé development. Thus, at mid-semester, students were favorable about their beginning process of developing the portfolio.

At the semester's end, students responded to a written questionnaire. Eighty-four percent (84%) of these students (N=19) indicated that the "portfolio improved their ability to integrate the varied parts of the social work learning experience." Among the most frequently cited benefits of the portfolio process, students said that (1) they were able to be organized in their field experience and could actually "see" their experiences and accomplishments, (2) they had a sharper focus, gaining clearer direction in their field placement experience, (3) they could be creative, and (4) they could use the portfolio for future job interviews. Some students used their portfolios as a tool in the mid-term and final evaluation sessions; others did not.

Most students said that they had to work on the portfolio on a regular basis (weekly). Students also felt that they needed to find a way to organize the portfolio early on in the development stage. If these two challenges were not met, the assignment became difficult. For example, if a student did not keep up with the development of the portfolio, he or she might not be able to access case materials later that would have demonstrated his or her skill development. One student learned the importance of safeguarding one's work when her portfolio was stolen from her car! She warned students to take precautions to protect their work.

How Field Instructors/Supervisors Feel About the Portfolio Approach

Field instructors and supervisors at CSU received a brief description of the portfolio approach at a field orientation program. In addition, a description of this model for student learning is in the BSW Field Manual (CSU, Andrus-Overly, 1996), though many field instructors do not get time to read through the vast amount of material in this manual. Several field instructors were unable to complete the evaluation survey, indicating that they have little knowledge about the portfolio approach. Some of these field instructors suggested that the social work program provide training on this particular model.

Fourteen (14) field instructors, representing 40% of the agencies having field students, completed an evaluation survey that was mailed to them. They identified benefits for the student's learning process and the student's ability to better understand social work practice and the social agency. These are important aspects for the initial generalist social worker (Schatz, Jenkins, and Sheafor, 1991).

Benefits for the Learning Process

Field instructors indicated that the portfolio approach was a practical and focused learning process, helping students to organize "what is often a somewhat chaotic experience," "combining school learning through collecting materials in field," and "offering a clarity through a visual, experiential learning assignment." Several suggested this approach encourages students' own creativity, promoting each learner's uniqueness. Further, this approach was seen to promote a self-learning style that allows students the opportunity for reflection in the learning experiences both close to the time of the learning, and later, as they use the portfolio to look back on and refer to later in their careers.

Promoting Opportunities to Better Understand Social Work and the Social Agency

Field instructors identified the importance of this approach in helping students to "integrate the theoretical with social work practice," putting, for example, the systems approach, the problem-solving approach, and solution-finding into view in a useful format. These field instructors felt that the approach offered the opportunity for students to begin to develop themselves professionally.

Least Positive Aspects of the Approach

Field instructors suggested that the portfolio process could become so time-consuming and such a primary focus for a student that the process itself might diminish the importance of the field learning.

Conclusion

Overall, the response by students and field instructors/supervisors to the portfolio was positive. This audience sees significant benefits in constructing a portfolio that allows students to gather information and examples of the new social worker's capabilities and competencies. In this process, a student gains greater insight into his or her personal and professional philosophy, field placement experience, and social work educational experience. The process serves as an important vehicle for self-reflective, self-evaluative practice.

The good news is that most students express very positive feelings when the portfolio is completed! In a few cases, students have used their portfolios in job interviews. These students report that they received very positive remarks from prospective employers about their portfolios. In this way, the portfolio exercise seems to ease the transition from student to professional.

Though a few concerns about this approach have been noted, these appear to be more logistical, such as the extent of portfolio content and student time pressures. With adjustments, the portfolio approach promises to be a useful tool in social work education and in the transition from student to professional.

References

Andrus-Overly, M. (1996). *BSW field manual.* Fort Collins, CO: Colorado State University, Department of Social Work.

Edgerton, R. (1991). *The teaching portfolio as a display of best work.* Paper presented at the AAHE National Conference on Higher Education, Washington, D.C.

Herr, K. (1992). *The teaching portfolio.* (Monograph). Fort Collins, CO: Colorado State ,Office of Instructional Services.

Schatz, M., Jenkins, L., & Sheafor, B. (1990). Milford redefined: A model of initial and advanced generalist social work, *Journal of Social Work Education, 26* (3), 217-231.

Schon, D. (1983). *The reflective practitioner: How professionals think in action.* New York: Basic Books.

27

Field Placement as a Building Block to Your Career

by Susan T. Ross, Ed.D., MSW, ACSW, LCSW

There are many ways to connect field instruction to a future career. At worst, it is one more hoop to jump through before getting the degree that will let you start your career. At best, it is the opportunity to integrate the knowledge gained in the classroom with real life situations. In between, there are many variations, probably at least partially dependent on the type of experience one is having in the placement.

In addition to using the internship experience as preparation for the skills needed in a career, the internship can also be used as the means to find out more about what you want from that career. This may seem strange, since you have already obviously decided on a career in social work. (Why else would you be going through all this work?) A social work education, however, creates the possibility of careers in a variety of social work practice areas. Field experience can be one opportunity to explore those many possibilities as you learn to put your education into practice.

Consider the internship experience an opportunity to make a dry run through the career development process. It is estimated that a person entering the job market today will change careers seven times. That means that you will probably have several opportunities to re-evaluate what you are doing and decide whether you want to continue or make a change. To assist you, there is a considerable amount of information available in career centers, libraries, and bookstores on career decision-making and the job search process. If you haven't already become familiar with this information in your decision to become a social worker, you may want to find it now.

The extent to which you can explore the career development process through your internship may depend on how your field assignment is made. Some programs assign internships with little input from the student, while others allow the student freedom to interview and select. Participate fully to whatever extent your school allows you to determine your actual placement or type of placement.

Use your internship and other sources of information to explore the following components of career development: self knowledge (interests, values, skills), the world of work (work settings, job market realities), and starting your career (job search tools, interviewing, finding the right fit).

Self Knowledge

The internship experience provides the perfect environment to increase your knowledge of yourself, particularly as it relates to your chosen career. Knowledge of self in the areas of *interests, values, and skills* provides the basis for a long, happy, successful career, regardless of what changes you make along the way. The matching of your talents, interests, and values with the requirements of a field of practice is the start of the career development process. Your career develops as your skills develop and you can participate more fully and at greater depths.

Part of knowing yourself is knowing where you are in the career development process. Are you beginning with your first professional career or are you coming from another career? Are you entering the profession after years of homemaking experience? Depending on your experience, you can take advantage of the internship to increase your knowledge of yourself and your potential to be satisfied within the profession of social work.

Interests are those things that arouse your curiosity and are frequently the primary attraction to a career. With what are you interested in being involved? In studying? In discussing with colleagues? What is the level or intensity of that interest? Is it a passing curiosity or something that you can enjoy exploring for many years?

Values guide you in your life. These are the ideas and beliefs you hold as important and use to make decisions about your behaviors. You want to find the career that uses similar values to make important decisions.

What is it about social work that interests you or seems to match your values? It may be the field in general or some specific area of it that has gotten your attention. Many people are attracted to social work because they want to help people or fight injustice. There are other professions that also work in these areas. What is it about social work that is different? Others are attracted because of a personal experience and having been helped themselves. Will helping others explore their issues be as rewarding as exploring your own issues?

Skills are those things you know how to do. They may be general or transferable skills, such as self-management (motivation, self-responsibility), communication (listening, writing), and interpersonal (building relationships, resolving conflicts). They may also be the specific skills associated with a particular job—for example, intake interviewing, charting notes, and therapeutic interventions. Skills are constantly being developed and updated throughout life.

What are the skills you already have and what new skills are you interested in learning? Some of these skills may be general personality traits or aptitudes, such as empathy, compassion, and intelligence. Others you may have learned in previous schooling and work experience. The internship will allow you to gain many more, but it will only be the beginning of a lifetime of acquiring and honing new skills.

Any placement you have, regardless of how well it matches what you think you want to be doing, can provide a rich opportunity to explore and develop interests, values, and skills. It may be helpful to create a list of the personal interests, values, and skills that are attracting you to the field of social work. Some of the career books have sample lists you can use as a guide. In whatever way your school lets you participate in the field placement selection process, seek out an opportunity that will let you explore and build upon the skills you already have.

Because social work students begin programs with varying degrees of skill development, you will want to be proactive in seeking new skills and not repeating what you already know. Use the lists you create to test for compatibility with the social work profession and specific practice areas.

The World of Work

The world of work consists of such topics as *job expectations, work ethic, work settings and job market realities*. The internship may be your first introduction to the professional world of work. You may have learned the basics of *work ethic* at part-time jobs and now need to build on those as you begin to build your professional reputation. Much of how you will be seen and known after graduation will begin with how you are perceived in your internship. You will be interacting with other professionals and you will probably be using your field instructor as a reference. Because you are a student, no one expects you to know everything, but you do need to practice ethically and to enter fully into the learning experience. The field placement is a safe place to find out what professional practice is all about with the guidance of your field instructor.

In addition to getting used to the professional role, or refining it if you are coming from another profession, the field experience is one of the best ways to learn about *job market realities*. In addition to your own placement, talk to other students about their placements. Talk to other social workers in your placement about their careers. You will want to join professional organizations such as the National Association of Social Workers, as a way to further explore career possibilities. The more you take these opportunities to explore possible *work settings* and meet other professionals, the better your chances of having a network in place when it comes time for job hunting. Most of all, this is the best opportunity you can get for "trying on a career" before you have to make a commitment. Take full advantage of the possibilities!

Starting Your Career

Two important tools in finding that first job out of school are the *résumé* and *good interviewing skills*. You may have had to use both to get your internship. If so, go back to those who selected you and get feedback on how you measure up to people they hire as social workers. You can also take the newest (or first, if you haven't been through the process) edition of your résumé to your field instructor and others responsible for hiring social workers. They may also be willing to do a mock interview with you to prepare you for the search.

Another key piece of finding the right position is *finding one that "fits" you.* Use your internship experience again to discover what a good fit is for you. Consider the different types of activities you do. What type of supervision works best for you? What is the atmosphere of the office? What is the philosophical and value base of the work? These are just some of the intangibles that can create either an ideal work situation or one of constant stress.

In summary, the field placement can be a rich source of information and learning above and beyond acquiring social work skills necessary for practice. Use it to build on your current skills, test out your interests and values, explore different social work careers, build a professional network, and practice the job search process.

For More Information

Powell, C. R. (1995). *Career planning today.* Dubuque, IA: Kendall/Hunt.

Lock, R. D. (1988). *Taking charge of your career direction.* Pacific Grove, CA: Brooks/Cole.

Kennedy, J. L., & Laramore, D. (1988). *Career book.* Lincolnwood, IL: National Textbook Company.

Bolles, R. N. (published annually since 1975). *What color is your parachute?* Berkeley, CA: Ten Speed Press.

Sinetar, M. (1987). *Do what you love, the money will follow.* New York: Dell.

28

10 Tips for the Transition—From Field Placement to Employment

by Althea Webb, MSSW, CSW

The first day of field seminar generates feelings of elation commingled with anxiety. There are overwhelming questions relating to "a good fit" with the profession, the agency and staff, and most of all with clients. The student intern is most often focused on passing (if pass/fail) or making an A (if graded) in the field practicum class. Once this mountain has been scaled, the student then takes a "much needed rest." This period of recovery may stretch into a year if the student has a comfortable, safe "student" job to continue to work while "waiting" for the professional job to materialize.

Here are ten tips to help you make the transition from unemployed or underemployed student to professional social worker. Five of the tips relate to preparing for employment during field placement or immediately after. The other five relate to being successful as a new employee. These tips are gleaned from students who have been successful in entering the job market over the last five years.

During or After Field Placement

1. Make a conscious effort to network during field placement.

I encourage students to identify and arrange informational interviews with community referral sources that their agency frequently works with. This assists the student in making referrals by putting a name with a face at the agency. This helps the student to better understand the services of related agencies. And this puts the student "out there," and community people know that you are a graduating social work student. Never underestimate the power of networking in producing job leads six months or a year down the road.

2. Have your agency field supervisor look over your résumé.

Prepare or revise your résumé early in the final semester. Talk to your agency field supervisor about how to describe your projected field placement experiences and opportunities. This will allow you to demonstrate your assertiveness skills by initiating a dialogue about expectations and opportunities for learning in field placement over the coming term. If your supervisor does not do the hiring at the agency, find out who does. Ask for suggestions about how to present yourself, ask about common errors seen on résumés sent in by applicants, and find out what the agency looks for in potential employees. A word of caution: do not indicate that you expect to be hired by the field agency, and don't beg the agency to hire you. Demonstrate a willingness to enter the job search arena, and ask the supervisor to keep you in mind if he or she hears of openings at other agencies. Do not expect to be exempted from the last few weeks of field if you secure a job offer. Always clearly indicate your availability date in your cover letter.

3. Use the college or university career services or placement office.

The primary mission of the career services office is to help students find employment. In other words, their job is to get you a job. Visit the office while still on campus full time, and get to know the staff that handle forwarding résumés to potential employers. Set up a placement file as soon as possible, and update the file as your situation changes. Plan to maintain your file after graduation.

4. Use an answering machine or voice mail during the job search process.

Make sure your message sounds professional. This is not the time to have a cute or irritating message telling folks to leave a message because you have gone partying. Check your message system often, and return calls promptly.

5. Stay in touch.

Maintain contact with classmates, the agency field staff, the university social work faculty, and the alumni office. A note or an e-mail message every so often will produce job leads as information becomes available about new services being developed in the community. You could become one of the first to know that individuals are moving from agency to agency. Always inform references that they may expect calls if you have recently applied for a "great" job.

Your First Job

Now, let's suppose you have your first professional social work job. The process of demonstrating your skills begins again. Here are five tips to help you be successful as a new employee.

1. Learn from the mistakes made in field placement.

Of course, you know what mistakes you made in field (many probably related to communication issues). Recall and learn from the mistakes that other students shared in the field seminar class. At this point, you are no longer a student, but you are still learning. Demonstrate that you are deeply committed to working with clients and that you are a team player.

2. Observe office politics from a distance.

You know that it takes time to understand the deeper issues going on with agency politics. Take time to learn the history of the organization. Also, take the time to observe and understand who the key players are in the organization. Do not ignore support staff. They may be your best allies in difficult situations. Be cautious about making fast and intimate friendships with people until you have had adequate time to really get to know them. You don't want to learn from the office secretary that your "best happy hour buddy" is on probation for ethics violations.

3. Establish a "happy file."

Employee satisfaction is often a key element in productivity. For the social worker, this may mean employee satisfaction will directly relate to the provision of effective client services. Social services agencies are often understaffed, under-funded, and seemingly over-utilized. Establish a "happy file" to review on an as-needed basis, to remind yourself that you, too, have inherent worth. Collect poems that inspire you, keep notes of thanks from clients, keep drawings that children have made for you, and keep copies of your positive evaluations. Be responsible for acknowledging your successes to yourself.

4. Stay put.

Try to stay on the first job at least one full year and preferably two to three years. Remember that there are no perfect agencies. Think seriously about moving your career in a particular direction, not just about changing jobs. You will soon learn that most social service community networks are a small group of dedicated people. Even in large urban areas, those who practice within a particular field know others within that field of practice at the other agencies. Try to enter the inner circle after you have "paid your dues," and guard your credibility, because it is your reputation.

5. Take your NASW *Code of Ethics* with you.

Never, never forget that you are a professional social worker. Live the *Code*, don't let it become "just something" you learned about in class. Too often, individuals get caught up in the daily tasks of work and forget why they entered the profession. Vow never to let this happen to you. Work at staying committed to the profession. Extend your student membership in NASW at the reduced transitional rate for new graduates. Attend the local meetings or start your own support group of dedicated social workers, and meet monthly over lunch or dinner.

Sound familiar? Maybe field placement really did teach you something about working in an agency setting. Only this time, there are no journals to write and turn in (late or otherwise). However, you will still have to write case notes! Having a successful field placement takes planning. The planning for field placement may have been primarily the responsibility of the university field coordinator and the agency field instructor. Now it is primarily your responsibility to plan for a successful career.

29

Welcome to the Brave New World of Social Work

Top 10 Tips on How to Survive and Thrive in the Profession

by Erlene Grise-Owens, Ed.D., LCSW, MSW

As a professional social worker who has been through various changes in the profession, I have seen some colleagues "burn out," while others thrive. I have observed particular survival and—to coin a new term—"thrival" strategies utilized by professionals who experience both longevity and satisfaction in their careers. I am grateful to all my colleagues who have helped me grow, survive, and thrive in my career.

I have compiled ten tips for thriving in our profession. I share this list with you, the new social worker, in hopes that you, too, can use this advice to survive and thrive in the demanding and wonderful field of social work. This list is in no order of importance, and is certainly not exhaustive of all the "thrival" strategies available to you.

1. Just because you have completed your degree, don't stop learning.

Anything that isn't growing becomes stagnant. Keep your professional life growing through continued learning. Participate in continuing education opportunities. Professional conferences, meetings, and workshops contribute to your knowledge base and build your professional network. Continuing education keeps you stimulated and growing, helping you to retain excitement and engagement with your profession.

Subscribe to professional journals—and actually read them sometimes. Block out time at work for delving into these readings or going to the library on a regular basis to do research on topics related to your work. Write about what you are doing, and add to the professional knowledge base through publications and presentations.

Consider pursuing an advanced degree—after you've paid off your first student loans, perhaps. Or think about the fact that you may not have to pay off those student loans right now if you go back to school. Whatever level you can do, commit to a continuing education plan.

2. Create and nurture peer support, mentors, and supervision.

Support systems are important in all arenas of life; social support systems in the work setting help social workers cope more effectively with stressful work conditions (Acker, 1999). Too often, new professionals isolate themselves either because the support network is not easily accessible or because they are so bogged down with the demands of a new career that they do not think they have time for this support. Often, social workers are in host settings, where they are the only social worker on staff. Although other professionals can provide wonderful support, creating a support network that includes other social workers is imperative—especially other social workers in similar roles in comparable settings (Ares, 1998). Peer support makes a critical difference in thriving in the profession (Baldino, 1998).

Sometimes new professionals feel the need to prove themselves as "competent" and are hesitant to ask for help, feedback, or support. Remember that every professional, regardless of his or her years of experience, needs to seek supervision and support. Seek out these resources. Learn more about how to use supervision; talk to your supervisor directly about what you need and how you work best. Part of responsible professionalism is using supervision appropriately and wisely.

In addition to peer support and supervision, be intentional about developing mentors, either in a formal or informal capacity. Remember that a mentor does not have to mentor you in every area. Rather, you may have a mentor for a specific facet of your professional development, and for a specific time period.

3. Remember the social work maxim: The client comes first.

Social workers face complex situations on a daily basis. Particularly in this era of managed care and privatization, it is often hard to maintain perspective regarding whose claim is priority. The multiple demands of insurance companies, agencies, other staff, or other systems' impinging needs and demands can lead to confusion. Unfortunately, this confusion can lead to succumbing to the pressure of shortchanging the client. When social workers lose this perspective, this can lead to discouragement and disenchantment about our purpose.

Obviously, the answers to the question of who exactly is the client and what is best for the client are not often simple or straightforward. However, the questions we ask determine to a great extent the answers we discover. So, the question of "What's best for the client?" is always a pivotal and clarifying one. This question helps us stay on track in a profession in which it is all too easy to become derailed. Remember our *Code of Ethics* and revisit this code regularly. Not only will the *Code* help you stay centered; it might also keep you from being sued.

4. Remember why you entered social work.

Students frequently ask, "Why isn't social work more respected? Why do we get paid so little?" The answers to these questions are complex. Certainly, this lack of respect and lower pay stems from what our society values, since (regardless of the rhetoric otherwise) our culture does not highly value helping people and pursuing justice. Working with the disenfranchised means social workers are linked inextricably with these populations; thus, we are devalued by association. Further, social work is a "female-dominated" profession, as are all "helping" professions. Female-dominated professions and helping professions tend to be under-valued and underpaid (Benokraitis, 1997; Headlee & Elfin, 1996).

Social workers' salaries remain low compared with other professions, including other female-dominated professions; this fact is particularly true for new social workers (Linsley, 1996). This lack of income and respect can lead to disenchantment and anger. These feelings can fester and leak out into our relationships with clients and colleagues. These feelings can lead to burnout. Certainly, we as social workers deserve to be paid more and respected more by our culture. We need to intentionally and intensively continue to seek this justice for our profession.

However, a key in retaining professional pride and integrity is to remember why you entered social work in the first place. If it was primarily to get rich, you were sadly misinformed and will quickly grow disenchanted with this profession. Rather, for many social workers, their entrance into the profession is a "calling." Or, as some colleagues attest, social work selected *them*. The profession of social work is rich in meaning and purpose. On a regular basis, revisit why you entered social work and reclaim that calling.

5. Social work is a broad field—you can change areas and still be a social worker.

Sometimes, in spite of our best efforts, we just get burned out with working with a particular population or particular area of social work. If you begin to feel constantly distracted, angry, disinterested, or discouraged, try some of the other tips in this list. If nothing you try seems to work, consider a change of scenery.

Social work is a big and broad profession, with many options. One of the reasons that some of us were attracted to social work in the first place is that, as a profession, it offers such variety. You can switch population groups, settings, and roles and still be a social worker!

6. Have a self-care plan—and actually DO it.

Remember the importance of the professional use of self. As social workers, our "selves" are our predominant tools. So, this "tool" must be honed, respected, and cherished. How well this tool is maintained and nurtured has a direct impact on how effectively we are able to do our jobs. Develop a specific self-care plan that addresses all areas of your life: physical, spiritual, mental, and emotional. Find ways to make this self-care plan a priority. Too often, social workers suffer from "compassion fatigue" because of becoming consumed by the cares of our careers. We cannot do it all. Be gentle, giving, and good to yourself. If you have trouble with doing that, seek out resources to help. *You* are too important to do otherwise.

7. Claim your identity as a social worker.

Often, the general public does not understand the profession of social work or the distinctions between "doing good," social services, and the profession of social work. Thus, sometimes it is tempting to say, "I'm a therapist" or some such title that is frequently better understood and more respected. However, as social workers, we must advocate in whatever ways we can for the profession of social work. Advocacy begins with you and me naming ourselves as social workers. Say "I am a social worker." Say it often and with professional pride.

8. Contribute to the profession.

Part of sustaining ourselves in our individual careers is sustaining the profession of social work as a whole. Give back to your profession. Contribute to the profession's growth. Join professional organizations and serve in whatever capacity you can.

Join your alumni group. Give back to the school that contributed to your education. If your alumni group is not active, inject some energy to enliven it. You don't have to take a large role, but do take a role.

Remember how important it was for you to have people in your life who mentored you as a student. Give back. Mentor a student. Many field supervisors state that a primary reason they do field supervision is because of the energy students infuse into the organization. Serve as a field instructor, or, if you are in a position to do so, hire students and support them in their educational endeavors.

As mentioned earlier, contribute to the profession by writing and presenting about what you are doing in the field.

Find others who want to write or present, and collaborate with them. Often, university faculty are excellent resources for co-writing/co-presenting or giving you suggestions regarding publications.

Contributing to the profession strengthens the whole profession. Thus, you as an individual social worker reap the benefits, as do all social workers. Think of the big picture and how you can do your part to keep our profession strong—for us, for future social workers, and, most importantly, for the clients we serve.

9. Keep a sense of humor and a sense of perspective.

The work we do as social workers is sometimes dangerous, dirty, and disrespected by many in the general public. Often, we are underappreciated and underpaid. However, we have the gift of working with the real issues and we are faced daily with the reality of the human condition. This can be overwhelming and discouraging, or it can be the opportunity to realize both the goodness and fragility of the human condition. It can be the opportunity to develop a rich sense of irony. Best of all, it can offer ample opportunities to see just how ridiculously funny we all can be at times.

Look for humor. Share stories. Play. Cry when you feel like it. Laugh as often as you can. Enjoy the incredible gift of being a part of a career that pays us to work at peace, justice, and bettering the world—and have some fun while doing it.

10. Develop your own unique "thrival" strategies.

This is an "incomplete" list, because to some degree, you must personalize your "thrival" strategies. Decide what strategies work for you and be committed and intentional in implementing them. Now, go and be the best social worker you can be.

References

Acker, G. M. (1999). The impact of clients' mental illness on social workers' job satisfaction and burnout. *Health and Social Work, 24* (3), 112-119.

Ares, M. (1998). When you're the only social worker. *The New Social Worker, 5* (3), *23-24.*

Baldino. R. G. (1998). The importance of peer support for the new social worker. *The New Social Worker, 5* (2), 18-19, 29.

Benokraitis, N. (Ed.). (1997). *Subtle sexism: Current practice and prospects for change.* Thousand Oaks, CA: Sage.

Headlee, S., & Elfin, M. (1996). *The cost of being female.* Westport, CT: Praeger.

Linsley, J. (1996). Salaries for new social workers—how much will I make? *The New Social Worker, 3* (1), 14-15.

Afterword

Ode to a Practicum Student

by Cheryl Waites, Ed.D., MSW, ACSW

You began this journey with fears and excitement
as you entered your field work class.
You wondered, "Can I interview a client, write a social history,
will I have money for gas?"

You met with your field instructor on that wonderful
yet difficult first field placement day.
Somehow you knew that if you stuck with him or her
your fears about this milestone would quietly go away.

You listened carefully because you knew
independence and your caseload would come soon.
So you shadowed your field instructor on home visits, team meetings,
whoops, even to the restroom.

Then it was time to meet your first client, you were excited,
self-conscious, your stomach sank.
You thought, "Will I ask the tough questions and remember to say
you're feeling blank *because* blank *and you want* blank?"

Journal writing became a way of voicing "I'm stressed,
but I'm learning and growing, too!"
You reflected on your personal struggles because
this work was becoming important to you.

A broker, case manager, advocate,
a social work generalist in action.
You saw complex issues, no easy answers,
the conflict, ethics, coping and satisfaction.

You worked hard learning, growing and doing,
to make this field experience go your way.
Hope that your social work career will be as productive
as you begin on this graduation day.

Index